LIVING FREE
COURSE MANUAL

Published by: Sycamore Publications
P.O. Box 158
Gig Harbor, WA 98335

To order: Website: www.sycamorecommission.org
Email: info@sycamorecommission.org

ISBN 978-0-9828756-3-6

Editorial: Arlyn Lawrence, Gig Harbor, WA
Design: Brianna Showalter, Ruston, WA
Book Packaging: Scribe Book Company, Lawton, OK
Printed in the U.S.A. by Bookmasters, Inc., Ashland, OH

CONTENTS

ACKNOWLEDGMENTS

After several writing projects, I am convinced that the acknowledgment page in a publication can be the most important page in the book. The reader needs to know that a manual like this is so much more than just a collection of objective truths in print. It represents lessons discovered and learned in the context of life with a community of people—in this case, a community that has grown larger and larger as this book and its contents gain increased circulation around the world. It has been an amazing journey, to say the least.

There have been many people and churches along the way that shared in this process with us. Some of them broke ground as pioneers with us during the learning process. Some are leaders and church families who have discipled their people in these truths and have given us helpful feedback over the years.

Among the many, I particularly want to say thank you to the people who constituted our church family during the eventful years when we were first learning and applying these truths—you know who you are. Thank your for your forbearance, teachability, and faith. Your investment has borne much fruit for God's Kingdom, far beyond what any of us could have imagined at the time.

I also want to particularly thank Joe Rhodes of New Hope Church, Stuart Lees of Christchurch Fulham, Tim Humphrey of St. Barnabas Kensington, and Hugh and Ginny Cryer of Winchester Vineyard. Your dialogue and input was immensely helpful.

Arlyn Lawrence, you went above and beyond in your commitment to this project. I know it is because you are motivated by a heart that is committed to these life-giving truths. You have experienced the transforming power that these truths unleash in your life and family. You performed major surgery with every aspect of this project then worked with the precision of a watchmaker on the final product. Thank you for how you have given your heart, spiritual gifts, and skills to this project.

Blessings,

Mike Riches

INTRODUCTION

Inside of you there is another you. Hidden deep in your heart is a person whose character is everything you have ever thought you could be and more. This person is fearless, able to navigate through every storm of life. This person is compassionate, able to love all of humanity—from the broken to the brash to the boorish. This person is filled with joy, bringing life and hope to every situation he or she encounters. This person speaks the truth, knowing that in a world in need of direction, someone must courageously point the way.

This person that resides in you is YOU—the real *you*, the *you* that God, your Creator, created you to be. This is the person that, in your heart, you are crying out to be. However, because we live in a world of sin—a world of pain, rejection, abandonment, violence, injustice, abuse, disappointment, and intimidation—this person God created you to be has been compromised and imprisoned. Facing such oppressors as fear, depression, anger, and sorrow, YOU have been held captive. But Jesus has come to set YOU free of those things that have held you prisoner. His freedom has come to release YOU to a life full of joy, compassion, love, and courage—a life of experiencing God's presence and power.

"Freedom" is at the heart of the life and message of Jesus Christ, and the mission of His followers. That is what this course is about—to help you identify where, why, and how you live in bondages and slavery instead of in freedom and hope. Through Christ's power, you can break out of those bondages to live in the freedom Jesus purchased for you. Jesus said, "You will know the truth, and the truth will set you free...if the Son sets you free you will be free indeed" (John 8:32). The Apostle Paul reiterated, "It is for freedom Christ has set us free" (Galatians 5:1).

"Freedom" is what this course is about. Think of it not merely as a course, though, but as a life experience that will give you skills and spiritual weapons for a lifetime of freedom if you will give yourself fully to the biblical truths you will discover. So, let the adventure begin!

> "Freedom" is at the heart of the life and message of Jesus Christ, and the mission of His followers.

SECTION ONE
Created with a Purpose

Notes: _____

_____

_____

_____

_____

_____

_____

_____

_____

_____

_____

_____

_____

_____

_____

_____

_____

_____

GOD'S ORIGINAL DESIGN

God's original design is that we would live eternally with Him in perfect unity and fellowship—with no sorrow, no pain, no hurt, and no sickness. He planned for us to live without relational tension, heartache, sorrow, or emptiness. Instead, we were created to be fulfilled, complete, joy-filled, and at peace. God created mankind to dwell with Him.

GOD CREATED US FOR A LOVE RELATIONSHIP WITH HIM

Genesis 2:15
The LORD God took the man and put him in the Garden of Eden to work it and take care of it.

God created us to live with Him in the Garden of Eden. He created mankind and each one of us for this type of relationship, dwelling with the God of the universe. In the Garden of Eden, man had unity and *intimacy* with God. God was able to lavish His love on Adam and Eve.

Take a look at the following verses and note God's great love for human beings—for each and every one of us.

Isaiah 54:10 (NIV)
"Though the mountains be shaken and the hills be removed, yet my unfailing love for you will not be shaken nor my covenant of peace be removed," says the LORD, who has compassion on you.

Zephaniah 3:17 (NIV)
For the LORD your God has arrived to live among you. He is a mighty savior. He will rejoice over you with great gladness. With his love, he will calm all your fears. He will exult over you by singing a happy song.

Each one of us has this kind of purpose—to love and be loved by God, to live out the assignments and purposes for which He has created us, to be loved by and to love other people, and to live without shame or condemnation in our lives.

GOD CREATED US FOR A PURPOSE

Genesis 2:15
The LORD God took the man and put him in the Garden of Eden to work it and take care of it.

Looking at Genesis 2:15 again, we also see that God had an assignment, or a purpose, for Adam: he was to work the garden and take care of it. God gave Adam responsibility and authority to make sure the garden (and, by inference, the whole world) was well taken care of. Throughout Scripture there are many examples of God's assignments and purposes for specific individuals.

GOD CREATED US TO LIVE FREE

Genesis 2:25
Now, although Adam and his wife were both naked, neither of them felt any shame.

Human beings were not created to live in shame and condemnation. Originally, there were not burdens or oppression in the world. There was not shame from personal experiences; there was not hurt in relationships. There was not defeat or opposition. There was a personal freedom. This was experienced in...

- Infinite selfless love
- Wholeness
- Significance
- Authority
- Intimacy with God
- Joy
- Purpose
- Worth
- Light
- Peace
- Security
- Life

ARE WE LIVING IN GOD'S ORIGINAL DESIGN FOR OUR LIVES?

If we take a realistic look at our lives and at the world around us, we see a world that has gone wrong, not a picture reflecting God's original design. On the individual, family, community, national, and international level we see death, murder, wars, and disasters. The landscape is filled with abuse, neglect, and hurt. Lives are filled with sadness, sorrow, emptiness, futility, and fear.

We were created to be fulfilled, complete, joy-filled, and at peace. God created mankind to dwell with Him.

Notes:

Human beings were designed to grow on a foundation of love and truth. Whenever these are missing or distorted in some way, the effect is a variety of behaviors or "postures" that push God's love and truth out of alignment. These can build up a wall of resistance, enmeshed within our personalities, which then actively resists the truth that can and will set us free. It also inhibits our ability to live in God's original design and purpose for our lives.

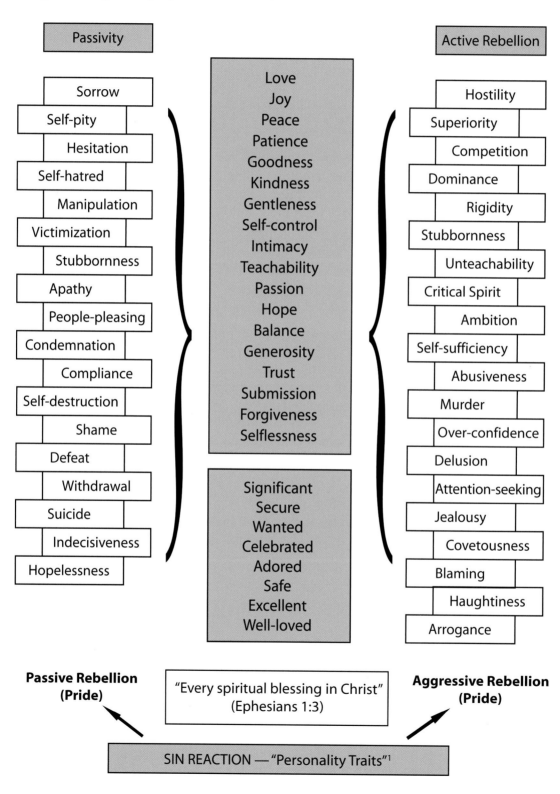

Passivity		Active Rebellion
Sorrow	Love	Hostility
Self-pity	Joy	Superiority
Hesitation	Peace	Competition
Self-hatred	Patience	Dominance
Manipulation	Goodness	Rigidity
Victimization	Kindness	Stubbornness
Stubbornness	Gentleness	Unteachability
Apathy	Self-control	Critical Spirit
People-pleasing	Intimacy	Ambition
Condemnation	Teachability	Self-sufficiency
Compliance	Passion	Abusiveness
Self-destruction	Hope	Murder
Shame	Balance	Over-confidence
Defeat	Generosity	Delusion
Withdrawal	Trust	Attention-seeking
Suicide	Submission	Jealousy
Indecisiveness	Forgiveness	Covetousness
Hopelessness	Selflessness	Blaming
		Haughtiness
		Arrogance

Significant
Secure
Wanted
Celebrated
Adored
Safe
Excellent
Well-loved

Passive Rebellion (Pride)

"Every spiritual blessing in Christ" (Ephesians 1:3)

Aggressive Rebellion (Pride)

SIN REACTION — "Personality Traits"[1]

If we are honest, we would probably say that there is something broken in our lives, our communities, our culture, and our world. Most would admit that we live in areas of bondage to our past, to our fears, and to our circumstances. What's broken? What happened to God's original design?

WHY DON'T WE LIVE IN GOD'S ORIGINAL DESIGN?

IT WENT WRONG!   Genesis 3:1-13

For Humans:
Adam disobeyed God. This disobedience caused Adam to give up his birth-right—to give up the right to live in God's original design. It had a dramatic impact not just on Adam but on every person in every generation that would succeed Adam.

Romans 5:12
When Adam sinned, sin entered the entire human race. Adam's sin brought death, so death spread to everyone for everyone sinned.

When we look at Romans 5:12, we see that each one of us in turn has inherited a sin nature, resulting in sin and a life lived outside of God's original design.

- Pride
- Hatred
- Insurrection
- Covetousness
- Selfish ambition
- Betrayal
- Deception
- Death
- Arrogance
- Rebellion
- Lies
- Murder

For Creation:
For many (if not most) of us who are from a Westernized culture, it is often difficult to comprehend the metaphysical and moral connection between humans and creation. The reality is that when Adam sinned, it not only brought a curse on Adam—all of humanity and all human cultures—but creation itself also fell under the curse of Adam's sin.

Romans 8:19-22
For all creation is waiting eagerly for that future day when God will reveal who his children really are. Against its will, all creation was subjected to God's curse. But with eager hope, the creation looks forward to the day when it will join God's children in glorious freedom from death and decay. For we know that all creation has been groaning as in the pains of childbirth right up to the present time.

Genesis lays out the consequences for this sin and disobedience to God:

SEPARATION FROM GOD

Each one of us has been separated from God. Isaiah 59:2 tells us, "Your iniquities (sins) have made a separation between you and your God." The sins we have committed have to be punished and the punishment is death. This death takes on various dimensions. Fundamentally, though, it is separation from the life of God that is found in relationship with Him.

Genesis 3:23
So the LORD God banished Adam and his wife from the Garden of Eden, and he sent Adam out to cultivate the ground from which he had been made.

The Scriptures tell us that there is fullness of joy in God's presence. Our sins separate us from that joy and that presence.

AUTHORITY OVER SATAN SURRENDERED

God created Adam to rule and govern the earth (Genesis 1:28). He created him in His own image and gave him authority over everything Jesus had made. Satan at this time was under Adam's authority. Satan, through deception, caused Adam to agree with him and submit to him against God. In so doing, Adam handed to Satan the keys of authority over mankind and this world.

Psalm 8:4-6
What are mere mortals that you should think about them, human beings that you should care for them? Yet you made them only a little lower than God and crowned them with glory and honor. You gave them charge of everything you made, putting all things under their authority.

John 12:31
The time for judging this world has come, when Satan, the ruler of this world, will be cast out.

The Scriptures tell us that there is fullness of joy in God's presence. Our sins separate us from that joy and that presence.

LACK OF PURPOSE

In Genesis 2 we see that God gave Adam an assignment of stewardship and oversight of His creation. Now Adam's life seems purposeless or futile—coming from dust and returning to dust. He is cursed by God to work hard in futility.

Genesis 3:19
All your life you will sweat to produce food, until your dying day. Then you will return to the ground from which you came. For you were made from dust, and to the dust you will return.

PERSONAL RELATIONSHIPS COMPROMISED

God's design for human relationships was for them to be among the greatest highlights of life. Instead there came contention between men and women—husbands and wives battling for control and casting blame. Sibling relationships became characterized by strife.

Genesis 3:12
The man replied, "It was the woman you gave me who gave me the fruit, and I ate it."

Genesis 3:16
Then he said to the woman, "I will sharpen the pain of your pregnancy, and in pain you will give birth. And you will desire to control your husband, but he will rule over you."

Genesis 4:8
One day Cain suggested to his brother, "Let's go out into the fields." And while they were in the field, Cain attacked his brother, Abel, and killed him.

PERSONAL BONDAGE

Genesis 3:8-10
Toward evening they heard the LORD God walking about in the garden, so they hid themselves among the trees. The LORD God called to Adam, "Where are you?" He replied, "I heard you, so I hid. I was afraid because I was naked."

Adam and Eve hid from God because they were afraid. Already, we start to see the consequences of sin. Fear and shame entered into Adam's existence, and he runs from God.

In Genesis 3:16-18, we also start to see a picture of pain and suffering. We start to see suffering in human relationships and in people's personal lives. For example, God's design did not include sorrow and pain in childbirth, nor did it include hardship and futility in making a living.

> God's design for human relationships was for them to be among the greatest highlights of life.

FULLNESS OF LIFE AND HEALTH WAS LOST

God's kingdom is one of vibrancy, life, and fullness of health. Sickness, disease, and death find their source in Satan's kingdom. Genesis chapter 4 is filled with death and murder, the result of sin. This was not how it was supposed to be. God did not design life to be filled with pain and suffering, heartache and sorrow, disease and death.

Genesis 3:16
Then he said to the woman, "You will bear children with intense pain and suffering."

HOW DO WE GET FREE?

How do we begin to walk out of the fallen state humanity finds itself in as a result of Adam's sin, and into the freedom God desires for us? Is there a special word to speak, a prayer to pray, or penance to perform? Sadly, many religious systems have sought to earn spiritual freedom by doing just that. But the reality is that living free starts with a person—Jesus Christ.

Throughout the New Testament we see it is only through Jesus Christ that we can be restored to our Heavenly Father. It is only through Him that we can experience real freedom in life through the power and love of God—a freedom God purchased for us at the great cost of the blood of His own Son:

Ephesians 1:7
He is so rich in kindness that he purchased our freedom through the blood of his Son, and our sins are forgiven.

We are lost and God's purpose for us has been lost. But this is not God's heart. God wants to restore His creation to its original design.

GOD SENT JESUS TO BUY OUR FREEDOM

God has made provision for mankind to take back what was lost. He has done this by sending His Son Jesus Christ to earth to die for our sins and bring us back into relationship with Him.

The Good News: Jesus Loves Us So Much, He Died for Our Sins

John 3:16 (NIV)
For God so loved the world that he gave his one and only Son, that whoever believes in him shall not perish but have eternal life.

John 10:10 (NIV)
The thief comes only to steal and kill and destroy; I have come that they may have life, and have it to the full.

We Need to Receive Jesus Christ as Lord and Savior

While God has done all the work necessary for us to receive salvation, there is a role that human beings have to play. We must engage in the process to receive this eternal life and believe to receive this new life through being born again. Then, and only then, can we begin walking in freedom.

John 1:12-13 (NIV)
Yet to all who received him, to those who believed in his name, he gave the right to become children of God—children born not of natural descent, nor of human decision or a husband's will, but born of God.

SALVATION IS COMPLETE LIFE RESTORATION

What was the purpose of Jesus' ministry?

Luke 19:10
For the Son of Man came to seek and to save what was lost.

When we receive Jesus Christ as Lord and Savior, we receive salvation; we are "saved." But what does this mean?

We get a fuller picture of salvation when we consider various forms of the Greek word *sozo* (translated "save" in Luke 19:10). This word communicates a more comprehensive understanding of salvation as restoration, healing, and making whole. These terms help us understand what Jesus had in mind when He came to minister salvation:

1. Restoration of Our Relationship with God

Romans 10:9
If you confess with your mouth, "Jesus is Lord," and believe in your heart that God raised him from the dead, you will be saved.

We are reunited with our Creator and are given the chance to live with Him throughout eternity. We are forgiven our sin debts. We are made whole in Jesus Christ and we recover intimacy with God.

2. Restoration of Our Purpose

Ephesians 2:10 (ESV)
For we are his workmanship, created in Christ Jesus for good works, which God prepared beforehand, that we should walk in them.

> The Greek word *sozo* (translated "save" in Luke 19:10) communicates a more comprehensive understanding of salvation as restoration, healing, and making whole.

We are also given a restored purpose; we begin to see that He has called each one of us for a great and mighty assignment. Just like Adam, God created each one of us with purpose. By His power and restoration we are given the chance to join Him again in His plan.

3. Restoration from Spiritual or Demonic Torment

Luke 8:36 (NIV)
And those who had seen it reported to them how the man who was demon-possessed had been made well.

Jesus heals the work of the enemy in our lives. He delivers us from oppression we may be experiencing. By His power we are able to escape the personal bondage caused by sin. He heals our emotions, mind, and will from our past experiences and hurts, and lead us to a life of freedom!

4. Restoration of Our Physical Body

Mark 10:52 (NIV)
And Jesus said to him, "Go your way; your faith has made you well." And immediately he regained his sight and began following Him on the road.

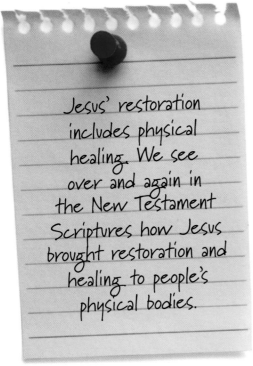

Jesus' restoration includes physical healing. We see over and again in the New Testament Scriptures how Jesus brought restoration and healing to people's physical bodies.

Jesus' purpose in salvation is to restore and empower the total person—spirit, soul, and body!

SALVATION IS IMMEDIATE AND ONGOING

Hebrews 10:14 (NIV)
For by that one offering he perfected forever all those whom he is making holy.

1. Understanding the Promises of Salvation

Scriptural salvation promises deliverance from the penalty of sin, the power of sin, and indwelling presence of manifested sin in our lives.

God sees you as your restored self TODAY!

2 Corinthians 5:17 (NIV)
Therefore, if anyone is in Christ, he is a new creation; the old has gone, the new has come!

2. Recognizing that Positionally Salvation Is a Finished Work; Practically, It Is an Ongoing Work

The fullness of Jesus Christ is deposited in us at salvation. We live our lives with His person, His character, and His image being released in our lives in increasing measures of righteousness, holiness, and love.

The Christian life is the process of growing into that freedom. We have a responsibility to "work out" our salvation.

Philippians 2:12 (NIV)
Therefore, my dear friends, as you have always obeyed–not only in my presence, but now much more in my absence–continue to work out your salvation with fear and trembling.

SALVATION—THE BEGINNING OF BEING RESTORED TO GOD'S ORIGINAL DESIGN[2]

2 Corinthians 5:17
This means that anyone who belongs to Christ has become a new person. The old life is gone; a new life has begun!

- Becoming a "new person" in Christ means that we are now able, by the Holy Spirit's empowering, to be the person God originally designed us to be.
- The Bible speaks to two degrees of original design—general and personal (see "The Christian's Birthright" on page 150 of this manual for examples of general original design).
- Some examples of original design are general indicators of God's design for all his children. Other examples are qualities unique to each individual.
- As He did with all of His creation, God created each person with purpose and a design. He created everyone uniquely, with gifts, skills, personality, and passions to specifically fulfill His purpose for that person's life.

Consider the story of Gideon in Judges 6. In this account, Gideon was hiding, living in fear. He thought of himself as insignificant and inferior in his family and community. He thought those "facts" were the truth about his life. How wrong he was! His self-perception was not in alignment with God's thinking. God's messenger spoke the truth that Gideon was *fearless*, a *leader*, a *warrior,* and a *mighty hero*. He was designed with great significance for his family, community, and most importantly God's kingdom! Knowing our original design will change our life forever if, like Gideon, we believe it and live it.

Another biblical example of original design is the birth of John the Baptist (see Luke 1:13-17). Read this account, too, and observe how specifically God spoke to John's parents about who he would be and what he would do.

Notes:

WHO, ME? (The Example of Gideon)

Read Judges 6:12-16.

Notice that God sent an angel to Gideon to awaken him to his original design. At the time of the angel's appearance, Gideon was threshing wheat in an underground cave because he was afraid of being discovered by his enemies. The angel called out to him, "Mighty hero..."

At the time, Gideon looked and felt like anything but a mighty hero! He responded, "How can I rescue Israel? My clan is the weakest... and I am the least in my entire family!"

It is important to understand that what God says about us is true whether or not we know it, see it, or accept it. If you continue reading in Judges, you'll see that God's words came true when Gideon finally accepted them and operated in them. But it wasn't until Gideon became aware of his original design that he was able to choose to live it out.

As we saw in the example of Gideon, a person's "original design" is not always visible to the naked eye. That's where prayer comes in. We can ask God to reveal to us, by revelation of His Holy Spirit, how He planned someone's personal original design. God wants us to know our original design. He speaks it to us through prayer and observation. He plants the truth of our original design deep in our hearts so that when we hear it, it resonates as true.

Components of personal original design may include a variety of characteristics, some of which are observable, some of which are only received through prayer. We should always check any impressions we receive in prayer against Scripture, testing that they are consistent with God's work and character. Consider some of the following aspects of (potential) original design:

- **Temperament** (characteristics of Jesus Christ such as compassion or justice, fruits of the Spirit, similarities to personalities of biblical characters)

- **Spiritual gifts** (gifts of mercy? Leadership? Encouragement? Exhortation? Prophecy? Wisdom? Discernment?)

- **Role** (if a man/husband, biblical qualities such as gatekeeper, provider, protector, strong leader, sensitive; if a woman/wife, biblical qualities such as helper-completer, mother's heart, nurturer, capable, gentle and quiet spirit, etc.)

- **Calling** (a leader like Moses or Deborah, a prophet like Samuel, a teacher like Paul or Priscilla, a friend like Jonathan, business-minded like Lydia, etc.)

However you receive it—whether on your own, in prayer, or through receiving original design prayer from a trained prayer team (if that is offered at your church)—listen, take note, and meditate on what the Lord reveals. Determine to see yourself more and more in your original design. *That* is the truth about who you are: not the past, not previous mistakes or failures, not even your successes and achievements. None of these things dictate or alter your original design.

2 Corinthians 5:14-16

Either way, Christ's love controls us. Since we believe that Christ died for all, we also believe that we have all died to our old life. He died for everyone so that those who receive his new life will no longer live for themselves. Instead, they will live for Christ, who died and was raised for them. So we have stopped evaluating others from a human point of view. At one time we thought of Christ merely from a human point of view. How differently we know him now (emphasis added)!

RESTORING WHAT WAS LOST—LIVING IN FREEDOM

"Living free" means appropriating all the blessings God intends for us in our salvation through Jesus Christ. It includes restoring God's original design and purpose to individuals, families, and churches. It also includes recovering our capacity for living with a sense of hope, significance, and fulfillment.

You'll gain insight about learning to live in freedom in the following chapters. But here's just a glimpse of what that means:

Freedom from Rejection

When Adam and Eve chose Satan's authority, they rejected God, resulting in separation from Him and from His presence of righteousness, goodness, and love. From that time on, rejection—and the living out of that rejection—became an integral part of the human existence. Rejection, in diverse expressions, now permeates our lives and relationships.

"Living free," in contrast, includes reconciliation with God and being fully accepted by Him in Jesus Christ!

2 Corinthians 5:18-19 (NIV)

All this is from God, who reconciled us to himself through Christ and gave us the ministry of reconciliation: that God was reconciling the world to himself in Christ, not counting men's sins against them. And he has committed to us the message of reconciliation.

Freedom from Guilt, Condemnation, and Shame

After Adam sinned, he hid from God because he felt *shame* (Genesis 3:7). He and Eve experienced guilt and condemnation for the first time. Without a redemptive relationship with Jesus Christ, we, too, live in the guilt, shame, and condemnation that our sin produces. Many times these cause us to live out all kinds of destructive behavior toward ourselves and others.

Notes:

Without a redemptive relationship with Jesus Christ, mankind lives in the shadow of death's gripping power and fear.

Living Free includes living forgiven for the guilt of our sin, living with peace toward God and man, and living without shame.

Romans 8:1 (ESV)
There is therefore now no condemnation for those who are in Christ Jesus.

Freedom from Fear and Anxiety

Another result of Adam's and Eve's sin was that they experienced *fear* (and fear's companion, *anxiety*) where they had previously enjoyed a sense of well-being, protection, provision, and personal care. Adam told God that when he heard Him approaching, he became afraid (Genesis 3:10). That had never happened before. Later, Adam and Eve's son Cain expressed to God his anxiety about feeling vulnerable and unprotected (Genesis 4:13-14).

That, too, had never happened before—it came from sin and has continued to plague the human psyche ever since. God's design is for us to live free of fear and anxiety.

Living Free includes learning to live a life of peace, confidence, and faith.

2 Timothy 1:7 (ESV)
For God gave us a spirit not of fear but of power and love and self-control.

Freedom from Insignificance and Futility

You are significant as a person and endowed with eternal purpose now that you are in Jesus Christ. You are filled with His glory; you carry His authority and you are saved to contribute to God's eternal purposes.

Living Free includes learning to live in the truth of your significance and eternal purpose as a person.

Colossians 2:9-10
For in Christ all the fullness of the Deity lives in bodily form, and you have been given fullness in Christ, who is the head over every power and authority.

Freedom from Slavery to Sickness and Suffering

Sickness, suffering, and death were not a part of God's original design for mankind. God can and does use it for His purposes and glorious objectives in our lives. But the coming of God's kingdom through the life, death, and resurrection of Jesus Christ includes the possibility of healing and the restoration of dignity to people through physical health.

Living Free includes learning to take up Jesus' authority over illness and disease.

Matthew 8:16-17 (ESV)
That evening they brought to him many who were oppressed by demons, and he cast out the spirits with a word and healed all who were sick. This was to fulfill what was spoken by the prophet Isaiah: "He took our illnesses and bore our diseases."

Freedom from Judgment and Fear of Death

Death was another result of Adam and Eve's disobedience. There are many dimensions of death—spiritual, physical, relational, and emotional. It is the final judgment of fallen humanity to be eternally separated from God—the ultimate death. Without a redemptive relationship with Jesus Christ, mankind lives in the shadow of death's gripping power and fear. While we all will die physically (unless Jesus returns first), the judgment and fear of death are conquered in Jesus Christ.

Part of Living Free is being released from the judgment and fear of death.

Hebrews 2:14-15 (ESV)
Since therefore the children share in flesh and blood, he himself likewise partook of the same things, that through death he might destroy the one who has the power of death, that is, the devil, and deliver all those who through fear of death were subject to lifelong slavery.

Freedom from Subjugation and Oppression by Satan

Jesus came to destroy the works of the devil and to disarm him in all his power and authority over mankind. We've seen that when Adam and Eve obeyed Satan and disobeyed God, they gave Satan authority and dominion over them. However, when Jesus Christ died on the cross and resurrected from death, He defeated sin and the power of sin's judgment. He destroyed Satan's authority and disarmed his power

Living Free includes living in and exercising our authority over Satan and his power over our lives.

Colossians 2:13-15
...Then God made you alive with Christ, for he forgave all our sins...In this way, he disarmed the spiritual rulers and authorities. He shamed them publicly by his victory over them on the cross.

1 John 3:8 (ESV)
The reason the Son of God appeared was to destroy the works of the devil.

MANKIND'S RESPONSIBILITY

HUMAN-DIVINE COOPERATIVE

This great gift of freedom is God's plan and work; it is dependent on Him and can only be accomplished by Him. We do not have the capacity to be as righteous as God is righteous, but we do have responsibility in the transaction of being saved and being freed from Satan's lies, schemes, and bondages.

This is what we describe as a "human-divine cooperative," *where a work that only God can do is initiated when a person exercises his or her God-given responsibility.* An example of this is the transaction of receiving salvation from sin as described in John 1:12: "But *as many as received Him*, to them *He gave the right* to become children of God, even to those who believe in His name" (emphasis added).

EFFECTING SPIRITUAL TRANSACTION IN REAL POWER NOT MERE WORDS

1 Corinthians 4:20 (NIV)
For the kingdom of God is not a matter of talk but of power.

Jesus Christ accomplished the work necessary for our forgiveness on the cross. There is a transaction that happens in the spiritual realm when we accept Jesus' finished work on the cross, when we pray a prayer for salvation. This power continues as we walk in obedience to Him. As we will learn later in this course, this transaction has far-reaching ramifications. As we look at the process of living in God's original design and freedom it is important to note the following:

1. We cannot receive freedom from self-help or positive thinking.
2. We cannot earn freedom or strive for it.
3. We cannot bring lasting change by sheer human will.
4. We cannot wish away our bondage.

WE NEED SPIRITUAL TRANSACTION!

UNDERSTANDING SPIRITUAL TRANSACTIONS

In day-to-day life, when a business deal is agreed upon, a contract is signed and then sealed by a notary of the public. Ownership or wealth is transferred and backed by the authority of the one guaranteeing it. Similarly, on a spiritual level, when a follower of Jesus Christ makes a determination of his or her will based on truth and makes a faith-filled declaration with his or her words, it is sealed by the ultimate Authority of the universe. The spiritual transaction is realized—it is done! A spiritual transaction takes place in the spiritual realm that has an impact in the natural or physical realm.

Components of a spiritual transaction:

- Agree with terms of God's truth.
- Submit to terms of God's truth.
- Make a faith-filled declaration with your words.
- Understand it is backed by God's sovereign authority.
- Know that a spiritual transaction has taken place with God's power released in every real way!

"Human-divine cooperative:" a work that only God can do is initiated when a person exercises his or her God-given responsibility.

SALVATION: THE INITIAL SPIRITUAL TRANSACTION

The good news is that the story doesn't end with what mankind and creation lost at the fall. Jesus Christ proclaimed that He had come "to seek and to save *what was lost"* (Luke 19:10, emphasis added). Note that this passage says Jesus came to seek and to save (restore, make whole) *what* was lost or *that which* was lost, not merely *who* was lost. Jesus came to initiate the work of restoration that begins with mankind's relationship with God, but goes beyond that to ultimately restore everything lost through Adam's sin.

To every place that Satan has sought to bring destruction, corruption, and bondage to sin, the life and ministry of Jesus Christ seeks to restore fullness, wholeness, and freedom. This restoration work will be ultimately completed in heaven, but our life of freedom certainly begins at salvation (Colossians 2:13-15).

The spiritual transaction of salvation is initiated when a person recognizes and responds to the following truths:

1. God Is Holy and Just; We Are Not

First you must recognize that God is holy and righteous and that you have not lived up to His standard of righteousness. Instead, we have all sinned against God and violated His person and truth. God is a just God and must, by His character, judge and punish sin and those who sin. Therefore, this places us in a place of God's eternal judgment, being separated from God for all eternity in a place of punishment.

Romans 3:10-12 (NIV)
As it is written: "There is no one righteous, not even one; there is no one who understands, no one who seeks God. All have turned away, they have together become worthless; there is no one who does good, not even one."

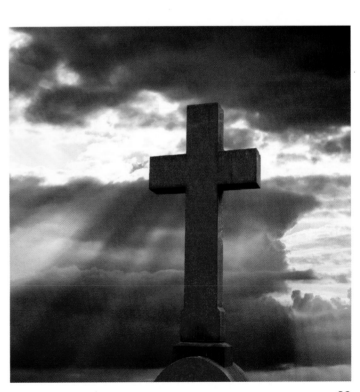

2. God Is Love and Sent His Son to Pay for Our Sin

Secondly, you must receive personally the truth that God is a God who is infinite in His love. In His great love for you He sent His Son, Jesus Christ, to earth to live life as a human being, which He did without sin. Then in His righteousness He innocently died on the cross. This was to pay for the punishment and penalty for mankind's sin against God so that God could justly forgive every man, woman, and child who would receive Him. Jesus then resurrected from death to demonstrate that He conquered Satan, death, and sin and satisfied God's justice toward sin.

Titus 3:3-5 (NIV)
At one time we too were foolish, disobedient, deceived and enslaved by all kinds of passions and pleasures. We lived in malice and envy, being hated and hating one another. But when the kindness and love of God our Savior appeared, he saved us, not because of righteous things we had done, but because of his mercy. He saved us through the washing of rebirth and renewal by the Holy Spirit.

3. We Receive New Life by Grace Through Faith and Confession

Thirdly, you need to exercise faith and, based on that faith, make some determinations and declarations with your will and mouth. If you believe the biblical truths shared here, you must act on them in prayer. If you do, you will be saved, forgiven of all your sin, and free to live eternally with God in heaven. You can begin to experience God's freedom, love, and power in your life.

Romans 10:9,10
For if you confess with your mouth that Jesus is Lord and believe in your heart that God raised him from the dead, you will be saved. For it is by believing in your heart that you are made right with God, and it is by confessing with your mouth that you are saved.

Romans 10:13 (ESV)
For "everyone who calls on the name of the Lord will be saved."

4. We Receive Jesus' Righteousness and Life

Fourthly, you exchange your sin for Jesus' righteousness. When God looks at you, He no longer sees your sin. Instead, He sees the purity of His own Son. That's because Jesus Christ, being righteous in nature and in life, was able to pay the penalty and cost of mankind's sin on our behalf. Consequently, in the spiritual transaction of salvation, through an act of faith, sinful people can exchange the guilt of their sin for Jesus' righteousness.

2 Corinthians 5:21 (ESV)
For our sake he made him to be sin who knew no sin, so that in him we might become the righteousness of God.

Have you unlocked the chain of spiritual death and received salvation by faith in Jesus Christ? If not, why not? You can pray to receive freedom right now! You simply need to:

1. **Admit** you are a slave to sin, separated from God and unable to save yourself.
2. **Confess** your sin to God and ask for His forgiveness.
3. **Believe** that Jesus' death on the cross and His resurrection from the dead paid the penalty incurred by your sin, and secured eternal life and freedom for you.
4. **Receive** God's forgiveness and freedom in faith, and begin to live in it. Determine that you now recognize Jesus to be the leader of your life, to whom you will submit and obey.

Ephesians 2:4-5
But God is so rich in mercy, and he loved us so much, that even though we were dead because of our sins, he gave us life when he raised Christ from the dead. (It is only by God's grace that you have been saved!

If you would like to be a restored child of God through faith in Jesus Christ, the following is a suggested prayer that you can pray, in authenticity and conviction:

Dear Heavenly Father, I believe that You are absolutely holy and just, and require that I be righteous with Your standard of righteousness. I also know and confess that I am a sinner and do sin. I have fallen short of Your holiness. I also believe that You are a God of love who sent Your Son, Jesus Christ, to die for the penalty of my sin. I believe that Jesus Christ is truly and fully God and, at the same time, also lived on earth truly and fully as a human being. I believe He lived and was without sin and absolutely holy. I believe that Jesus died on the cross to pay for the punishment of my sin and resurrected from death demonstrating He conquered sin and satisfied your judgment against my sin. In faith and by Your grace I ask You to forgive my sin and receive me as Your child, fully forgiven with the righteousness of Jesus Christ and restored to relationship with You. I receive Your forgiveness and declare that I will live a life continually seeking to turn from sin and live instead in joyful obedience to You as the Leader and Savior of my life. Amen.

SUBSEQUENT SPIRITUAL TRANSACTIONS

The foundational spiritual transaction in the Christian life is when a person receives Jesus Christ as his or her Lord and Savior. Based on truth, faith-filled words are spoken. A prayer is made with conviction from the heart, and a transaction takes place and is sealed by the power of God (Romans 10:9). We see the result of this with a changed life in the natural realm (2 Corinthians 5:17; Galatians 2:20).

In the spiritual transaction of salvation, through an act of faith, sinful people can exchange the guilt of their sin for Jesus' righteousness.

However, this is not the last spiritual transaction we make! We make subsequent spiritual transactions any time we enter into a human-divine cooperative through prayer. For example, a similar kind of thing happens with prayers of repentance—spiritual transactions take place that will have natural realm effects. In these transactions, we as humans initiate an action or activity to which God responds by doing what only He can do.

ENTERING INTO A LIFE OF FREEDOM

There are several strategic truths for walking the path of living free in the power and fullness in which God designed us to walk. We will address these truths more fully in future sessions, but here we will briefly look at one foundational truth. It will get us started so we can immediately begin our journey: the freedom found in the spiritual transaction of *repentance*.

UNDERSTANDING AND EXERCISING REPENTANCE

Mark 1:14,15 (NIV)
After John was put in prison, Jesus went into Galilee, proclaiming the good news of God. "The time has come," he said. "The kingdom of God is near. Repent and believe the good news!

Repentance Means to Stop, Turn, Walk in the Opposite Direction

To repent we:

Recognize our sin and confess it.

1 Corinthians 15:34 (NIV)
Come back to your senses as you ought, and stop sinning.

Renew our mind in the truth.

Romans 12:2 (NIV)
Do not conform any longer to the pattern of this world, but be transformed by the renewing of your mind. Then you will be able to test and approve what God's will is—his good, pleasing and perfect will.

Turn from our sin.

2 Timothy 2:19 (NIV)
Everyone who confesses the name of the Lord must turn away from wickedness.

Do the opposite.

Ephesians 4:21 (NIV)
He who has been stealing must steal no longer, but must work, doing something useful with his own hands, that he may have something to share with those in need.

PRAYING REPENTANCE

A prayer model that synthesizes the principles of James chapter four is what we call the "4-R's." This model can help us understand and apply the James 4 principles in a memorable and practical way.

Briefly, the 4-R's include (these steps will be examined in more detail in Section Five, "Dismantling Strongholds"):

1. **Repent** and receive the Lord's forgiveness.
2. **Rebuke** demonic influence and renounce the lies that contradict God's truth.
3. **Replace** the lie or sinful behavior with what is true and right, renew your mind in God's Truth, and live accordingly in actions of obedience.
4. **Receive** the infilling work of God's Spirit, and rejoice!

Note what repentance is *not*:

- it is not self-help
- it is not religious legalism
- it is not just hoping

- it is not mere positive thinking
- it is not striving
- it is not sheer human will

1 Corinthians 4:20 (NIV)
The kingdom of God … is a matter of power.

LIVING OUT REPENTANCE AS A LIFESTYLE

How do we go forward?

We start by understanding that …

… we are forgiven, accepted, and secure in Christ.
… our relationship with God is grace-based.
… we live and respond to Holy Spirit conviction, not condemnation.
… we never need withdraw from God—His forgiveness is immediate and complete.

SECTION TWO
One World, Two Realms

Notes: _____

_____

_____

_____

_____

_____

_____

_____

_____

_____

_____

_____

_____

_____

_____

_____

_____

_____

_____

OUR WORLD HAS TWO REALMS

The Bible teaches us that the world we live in has two realms—one that is physical and one that is spiritual. "Set your sights on the *realities of heaven*," the Apostle Paul wrote. "Let heaven fill your thoughts. Do not think only about things down here on earth" (Colossians 3:1-2, emphasis added). In one realm—the natural realm—we can easily use our five natural senses: we see with our eyes, we hear with our ears, we smell, we taste, and we touch. However, those same five natural senses do us little good in the other realm. We might say that one realm—the natural one—is material, and the other realm—the heavenlies realm—is invisible or spiritual.

But being invisible to the naked eye does not make the heavenlies realm any less "real." While these two realms are distinct, they operate simultaneously in our lives. How does that work? There are many accounts in Scripture that illustrate the reality of the two realms, but few as succinctly and comprehensively as that of Job.

JOB'S WORLD COLLAPSES

Job 1:13-19
One day when Job's sons and daughters were dining at the oldest brother's house, a messenger arrived at Job's home with this news: "Your oxen were plowing, with the donkeys feeding beside them, when the Sabeans raided us. They stole all the animals and killed all the farmhands. I am the only one who escaped to tell you."

While he was still speaking, another messenger arrived with this news: "The fire of God has fallen from heaven and burned up your sheep and all the shepherds. I am the only one who escaped to tell you."

While he was still speaking, a third messenger arrived with this news: "Three bands of Chaldean raiders have stolen your camels and killed your servants. I am the only one who escaped to tell you."

While he was still speaking, another messenger arrived with this news: "Your sons and daughters were feasting in their oldest brother's home. Suddenly, a powerful wind swept in from the desert and hit the house on all sides. The house collapsed, and all your children are dead. I am the only one who escaped to tell you."

Job 2:7-10
He struck Job with a terrible case of boils from head to foot. Then Job scraped his skin with a piece of broken pottery as he sat among the ashes. His wife said to him, "Are you still trying to maintain your integrity? Curse God and die."

But Job replied, "You talk like a godless woman. Should we accept only good things from the hand of God and never anything bad?" So in all this, Job said nothing wrong.

Note the nature of Job's misfortunes:

- His herds and servants were attacked by neighboring tribes and nations and hit by lightning—thus Job lost his ability to produce income.
- His children were killed by a weather disaster and his marriage was destroyed.
- He lost his health.

LOOK BEHIND THE SCENES OF JOB'S DISASTERS

Job 1:6-12
One day the angels came to present themselves before the LORD, and Satan the Accuser came with them. "Where have you come from?" the LORD asked Satan. And Satan answered the LORD, "I have been going back and forth across the earth, watching everything that's going on."

Then the LORD asked Satan, "Have you noticed my servant Job? He is the finest man in all the earth—a man of complete integrity. He fears God and will have nothing to do with evil."

Satan replied to the LORD, "Yes, Job fears God, but not without good reason! You have always protected him and his home and his property from harm. You have made him prosperous in everything he does.

The Bible teaches us that the world we live in has two realms—one that is physical and one that is spiritual. Being invisible to the naked eye does not make the heavenlies less "real."

God wants us to understand what is happening in the spiritual realm as well as the visible world.

Look how rich he is! But take away everything he has, and he will surely curse you to your face! "All right, you may test him," the LORD said to Satan. "Do whatever you want with everything he possesses, but don't harm him physically." So Satan left the LORD's presence.

Job 2:1-7
One day the angels came again to present themselves before the LORD, and Satan the Accuser came with them. "Where have you come from?" the LORD asked Satan. And Satan answered the LORD, "I have been going back and forth across the earth, watching everything that's going on."

Then the LORD asked Satan, "Have you noticed my servant Job? He is the finest man in all the earth—a man of complete integrity. He fears God and will have nothing to do with evil. And he has maintained his integrity, even though you persuaded me to harm him without cause."

Satan replied to the LORD, "Skin for skin—he blesses you only because you bless him. A man will give up everything he has to save his life. But take away his health, and he will surely curse you to your face!"

"All right, do with him as you please," the LORD said to Satan. "But spare his life." So Satan left the LORD's presence, and he struck Job with a terrible case of boils from head to foot.

Note the cause of Job's misfortunes:

- A superficial observation would give the impression that the misfortunes were merely physical, natural world issues.
- When we read the first two chapters of Job we realize the real source of Job's calamities was in another world, a world that is spiritual and invisible.

"SPIRITUAL P.I.P." (PICTURE-IN-PICTURE)

You have probably seen television screens with more than one screen simultaneously in view, allowing you to watch multiple shows or events at one time. This feature is sometimes called "picture in picture." With a "p.i.p." television, you can watch a news show and a baseball game at the same time.

With tools like this available to us, the Western world has increasingly become a technologically-savvy culture of multi-tasking—or keeping more than one thing in view at a time. The same is not necessarily true spiritually. Sensitivity to the spiritual realm is a quality that has largely been lost in our pursuit of the empirical, rational, and technical.

- If we were only capable of seeing life from a single dimension, it would be easy to say that Job suffered from a string of great misfortunes. However, the Scriptures make it clear that activity in the spiritual realm directly influenced Job's life on earth.

- God wants us to understand what is happening in the spiritual realm as well as the visible world. A modern example of this is the "picture-in-picture" capability of a television that allows the viewer to see what is happening on two different channels at the same time.

ONE WORLD, TWO REALMS:

The Apostle Paul wrote of this realm often, and it is a central theme in his letter to the Ephesians. He mentions "the heavenlies" five times, using the specific New Testament word *epouranios* to refer to this realm (Ephesians 1:3, 26, 2:6, 3:10, 6:12).

"The Heavenlies" (Invisible Realm of the Spirit)

This realm includes all that is spiritual, invisible, or not seen in the natural (God, Holy Spirit, angelic beings, demonic beings, curses, and blessings).

"The Natural" (Visible Realm of the Material)

This realm includes all that can be perceived by the natural senses in the physical world.

Both realms are completely real, and events in one bear directly on events in the other.

THE INTERRELATIONSHIP OF THE TWO REALMS

How do we see the two realms interface? What does this look like in real life? Daniel 10:2-21 presents a graphic insight concerning the interfacing of the two realms. The statesman and prophet Daniel had been passionately praying and seeking God's face concerning Israel's future. There was no apparent response to his prayers for three weeks; nothing seemed to be happening. But in reality, a fierce war was raging in the heavenlies.

WHAT TRANSPIRES IN THE HEAVENLIES AFFECTS THE NATURAL REALM

Daniel 10:2-13 (NIV)
In those days I, Daniel, had been mourning for three entire weeks. I did not eat any tasty food, nor did meat or wine enter my mouth, nor did I use any ointment at all, until the entire three weeks were completed. And on the twenty-fourth day of the first month, while I was by the bank of

Heavenly Realm

Our World

Natural Realm

> We cannot afford to be ignorant or to ignore this reality. We live in one world—but it does have two realms and we live in both of them.

the great river, that is, the Tigris, I lifted my eyes and looked, and behold, there was a certain man dressed in linen, whose waist was girded with a belt of pure gold of Uphaz. His body also was like beryl, his face had the appearance of lightning, his eyes were like flaming torches, his arms and feet like the gleam of polished bronze, and the sound of his words like the sound of a tumult. Now I, Daniel, alone saw the vision, while the men who were with me did not see the vision; nevertheless, a great dread fell on them, and they ran away to hide themselves. So I was left alone and saw this great vision; yet no strength was left in me, for my natural color turned to a deathly pallor, and I retained no strength. But I heard the sound of his words; and as soon as I heard the sound of his words, I fell into a deep sleep on my face, with my face to the ground. Then behold, a hand touched me **and set me trembling on my hands and knees. And he said to me,** "O Daniel, man of high esteem, understand the words that I am about to tell you and stand upright, for I have now been sent to you." And when he had spoken this word to me, I stood up trembling. Then he said to me, "Do not be afraid, Daniel, for from the first day that you set your heart on understanding this and on humbling yourself before your God, your words were heard, and I have come in response to your words. But the prince of the kingdom of Persia was withstanding me for twenty-one days; then behold, Michael, one of the chief princes, came to help me, for I had been left there with the kings of Persia."

Note what was taking place:

Daniel 10:20-21 (NIV)
Then he said, "Do you understand why I came to you? But I shall now return to fight against the prince of Persia; so I am going forth, and behold, the prince of Greece is about to come. However, I will tell you what is inscribed in the writing of truth. Yet there is no one who stands firmly with me against these forces except Michael your prince."

- The Greek Empire came on the scene about 200 years later but its arrival was preceded by a spiritual battle in the heavenlies.
- Daniel's prayers prompted the commissioning of an angel by God and the ensuing battle between spirit princes in the heavenlies.
- From this account we can see that what takes place in the natural realm is a result of what has and is taking place in the heavenlies.
- There is indeed an interfacing of the two realms that goes on in this world—even over your life, family, culture, community, nation, and church.

We cannot afford to be ignorant or to ignore this reality. We live in one world—but it does have two realms and we live in both of them. We must learn to ask questions such as:

- Is this difficult situation "just happening"?
- Is my bad mood "just happening?"
- Is my strained marriage "just happening?"
- Is oppressed corporate worship due merely to weather and the seasons?
- Why does a selfish and stingy spirit (or one of division, rebellion, etc.) persist in the church from generation to generation?
- Is a persistent lack of joy and zeal due merely to personality?
- Are bigotry, prejudice, and ethnic cleansings "just happening?"
- Is bad health "just happening?"
- Are wars "just happening?"
- Are famines "just happening?"
- Are financial downturns "just happening?"
- Is depression "just happening?"

JESUS' LIFE AND MINISTRY READILY RECOGNIZED BOTH REALMS

Jesus' life was characterized by living readily and alertly to both realms. It seemed as though at every turn He encountered demonic beings. Jesus recognized that often what appeared to be issues of the natural realm were in actuality spiritual in nature. He understood the power of the spoken word in healings, blessings, and curses.

Luke 4:40-41
When the sun was setting, the people brought to Jesus all who had various kinds of sickness, and laying his hands on each one, he healed them. Moreover, demons came out of many people, shouting, "you are the Son of God!" but he rebuked them and would not allow them to speak, because they knew he was the Christ.

Luke 8:24
The disciples went and woke him, saying, "Master, Master, we're going to drown!" He got up and rebuked the wind and the raging waters; the storm subsided, and all was calm.

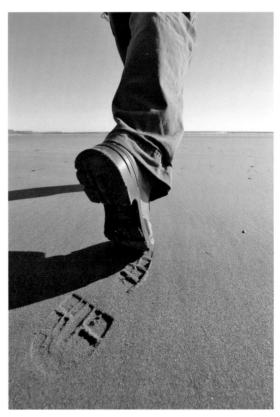

Jesus, of course, encountered Satan personally in a 40-day battle during His temptation in the wilderness (Matthew 4). He had a demonic encounter at His first synagogue sermon in Capernaum (Mark 1). His ministry included releasing people who were captives to demonic activity and identifying such activity as part of God's Kingdom coming to earth (Luke 11). A significant reason for Jesus coming to earth was, in fact, to destroy the works of the devil by His death and resurrection (Hebrews 2).

THIS WORLD IS A WAR ZONE

Intellectualism is a central reason for the weakness of the church today in the West, causing it to live in a worldly manner with natural realm thinking and strategy.

Part of living free is experiencing a restoration of our ability to be sensitive to both the heavenly and natural realms at the same time. We need to develop an appreciation for how the two realms interface with one another. We live in a very spiritual world with spiritual powers. We live in a war zone fundamentally and primarily fought in the spiritual or heavenlies realm. We live in the middle of a cosmic battle originating in the heavenlies but which has far reaching effects in the natural realm.

Ephesians 6:12 (NIV)
For our struggle is not against flesh and blood, but against the rulers, against the powers, against the world forces of this darkness, against the spiritual forces of wickedness in the heavenly places.

Ephesians 6:12
For we are not fighting against people made of flesh and blood, but against the evil rulers and authorities of the unseen world, against those mighty powers of darkness who rule this world, and against wicked spirits in the heavenly realms.

We Cannot Afford to be Ignorant of This Battle

John 10:10 (NIV)
The thief comes only to <u>steal</u> and <u>kill</u> and <u>destroy</u>; I have come that they may have life, and have it to the full (empasis added).

1 John 3:8 (NIV)
He who does what is sinful is of the devil, because the devil has been sinning from the beginning. The reason the Son of God appeared was to destroy the devil's work.

2 Corinthians 2:10-12 (NIV)
If you forgive anyone, I also forgive him. And what I have forgiven–if there was anything to forgive–I have forgiven in the sight of Christ for your sake, in order that Satan might not outwit us. For we are not unaware of his schemes.

CHRISTIANS MUST LIVE IN REALITY OF THE SPIRITUAL REALM

We, as Christians, are to live wisely and fearlessly in the reality of the spiritual realm. Scripture clearly states that Christians are to continue living out the life and ministry Jesus modeled for us (John 17:18, 20; 20:21). The Apostle Paul taught that we are in a spiritual war (Ephesians 6:12).

1. has been delivered from the dominion of darkness.

Colossians 1:13-14
For he has rescued us from the dominion of darkness and brought us into the kingdom of the Son he loves, in whom we have redemption, the forgiveness of sins.

2. has the promise of great power by being indwelt by God.

1 John 4:4
You, dear children, are from God and have overcome them, because the one who is in you is greater than the one who is in the world.

3. has received authority through Jesus Christ over demonic beings and their influence.

Luke 10:17-19
The seventy-two returned with joy and said, "Lord, even the demons submit to us in your name." He replied, "I saw Satan fall like lightning from heaven. I have given you authority to trample on snakes and scorpions and to overcome all the power of the enemy; nothing will harm you."

Ephesians 2:6
And God raised us up with Christ and seated us with him in the heavenly realms in Christ Jesus.

THE WESTERN MINDSET IS RESISTANT TO THE BIBLICAL / JESUS' WORLDVIEW

- There is over-reliance on the five senses as well as the crippling effects of humanism and rationalism.
- There is a dismissal of demons or controlling spiritual powers as "primitive."
- There is a vast influence of intellectualism in people's worldviews and mindsets.

This is a central reason for the weakness of the church today in the West, causing it to live in a worldly manner with natural-realm thinking and strategy.

Humanistic Rationalism

Sometimes when you live in the midst of a culture or mindset it is difficult to see all of its characteristics. We don't realize how much a particular worldview influences how we see life and think.

Notes: _____

The following diagnostic is designed to help you discern if you are overly influenced by Western rationalism or influences of the enlightenment that would inhibit you from living with a biblical worldview toward the spiritual realm. Check all that apply:

- ❑ I like to see things in a logical way and struggle to embrace the unempirical and/or the seemingly illogical.
- ❑ I consider people who believe and live with consideration toward angels and demons, blessings and curses, to be "extreme."
- ❑ I look first for logical and natural reasons for the cause of a problem before asking for the Holy Spirit's wisdom and understanding.
- ❑ I have valued and relied on my mind, reason, and intellectual capacity to see me through life.
- ❑ I often find it hard to see with "the eyes of faith." I easily become despondent because I underestimate the power of God to bring change.
- ❑ My family places a high value on thinking logically and clearly and on having good, solid, empirical reasons for thinking or believing something.
- ❑ I think I understand that much of the battle is "spiritual" in nature, but I am more comfortable working out a solution than asking God to see the situation from His perspective.
- ❑ I struggle to believe that the invisible realm is real and influential on a daily basis.
- ❑ I can't seem to fully grasp all that surrounds the "heavenly realms" and so don't give it much attention.
- ❑ I think the idea of demons and angels is all a bit primitive, superstitious, and/or irrelevant.
- ❑ Surely all I need is to "understand the Word" and to live it. The supernatural realm is not my responsibility.

IMAGINE A CHURCH, FAMILY, OR COMMUNITY WHERE:

- no one is holding a grudge against another.
- no one is hiding from others due to fear of rejection.
- no one is drawing back from God-given challenges for fear of failure.
- no one is hiding their gifts because of their own sense of inadequacy and insignificance.
- no one is fearful of the enemy.
- no one is subdued by worshiping the idols of money, sex, and power.
- no one is trapped by the fear of man.
- no one is withholding his or her resources.
- no one is stuck in passivity and apathy.
- all are standing up in spiritual power and authority, living real lives and committed to the flourishing of others.

This is the purpose of Jesus' ministry among us today!

WE LIVE IN BOTH REALMS SIMULTANEOUSLY BY THE HOLY SPIRIT

God has provided all we need to live in power in both realms. God, by His divine power, has given us all we need for life and godliness (2 Peter 1:3). The foundation of this, of course, is found in our salvation in Jesus Christ. But He also has provided us with a relationship with the Holy Spirit that allows us to operate in God's divine power in the natural realm.

Without the Holy Spirit's power, we would be unable to fully follow Jesus Christ in our daily lives. We would be unable to live in obedience to all God asks of us, or to live triumphantly over Satan and his schemes. Without His power, we would not be able to carry out the mission and ministry of Jesus Christ. Being filled with the Holy Spirit is what enables us to live in freedom, be restored to God and His design for us, and carry out the life and ministry of Jesus.

The Empowering of the Holy Spirit Is Necessary and Is a Command to the Believer.

- In order to live a life that tears down strongholds, it is an absolute *necessity* to be filled with God's Spirit. Likewise, in order to live in obedience to God, we are *commanded* to be filled with God's Spirit.

- Ephesians 5:18 commands us to continually live life filled with the Holy Spirit.

Ephesians 5:18 (NCV)
Do not be drunk with wine, which will ruin you, but be filled with the Spirit.

- We are to continually live life in the fullness of the Holy Spirit, always seeking to *increase* His fullness in our lives.

We Should Live Open and Ready for an Extra Measure of Holy Spirit Filling

- All of us receive the Holy Spirit at salvation.

- There are times when our life demands resisting a distinct temptation to live in holiness or offers an opportunity to minister for God. We need the power of the Holy Spirit in a distinct and powerful manner that is beyond the ongoing measure of living being filled with God's Spirit. For example, the Apostle Peter lived in a state of Holy Spirit filling from Pentecost on, but yet he received *extra-measure filling several times*, as did other believers.

Acts 4:8

Then Peter, <u>filled with the Holy Spirit</u>, said to them, "Rulers and elders of the people..." (emphasis added).

We could describe this as an empowering or an *anointing*.

You Should Not Seek out Manifestations. What You Should Seek is the Holy Spirit to Help You:

- experience deeper intimacy with God and His ways.
- be flooded with His love, joy, and the fruit of the Spirit by knowing Him more intimately.
- be triumphant over sin by more fully experiencing the power of His resurrection in your life.
- be bolder in your witness by more fully experiencing the power of His resurrection in your life.
- live out the life and ministry of Jesus Christ.
- supernaturally minister so as to bear increasingly more spiritual fruit by more fully experiencing the power of His resurrection in your life.

In all this, it is important to understand that Holy Spirit infilling is born out of relationship with God and lifestyle.

Don't Have Unrealistic Expectations

Holy Spirit filling can be different between individuals and situations. There are distinct expressions and releases of the Holy Spirit through-out your life-long walk with God that mark you and consequently bring distinct changes to your life.

- There will most likely be combinations of several expressions of Holy Spirit filling in your life.
- Many times an infilling of the Holy Spirit is realized in a season of suffering when you abandon yourself to God.
  - It can include a distinct spiritual, emotional, and/or physical experience.

Holy Spirit filling typically includes a gradual steady release through consistent exercise in God's Word, prayer, and obedience. Theologian Wayne Grudem provides an analogy to illustrate being filled with God's Spirit by comparing it to the filling of a balloon in contrast to filling a glass with liquid. The liquid cannot expand the volume capacity of the glass, but increased air can increase the volume capacity of a balloon. So it is with our lives: as we are increasingly filled with God's Spirit our capacity to live out the supernatural life and power of God increases.[1]

38

D.L. Moody (an evangelist used by God in the 1800's) was one who experienced a distinct work of the Holy Spirit subsequent to his salvation, which he called the *baptism of the Holy Spirit*. He said,

One day, in the city of New York—oh what a day—I cannot describe it, I seldom refer to it; it is almost too sacred of an experience to name. Paul had an experience of which he never spoke for fourteen years. I can only say that God revealed Himself to me, and I had such an experience of His love that I had to ask Him to stay His hand. I went to preaching again. The sermons were not different; I did not present new truths, and yet hundreds were converted. I would not now go back where I was before the blessed experience if you should give me all the world.

It is only through the Holy Spirit you will live free in a supernatural life, fully engaged in both the heavenly and natural realms!

Prepare Yourself to be Filled with the Holy Spirit

Being filled with the Holy Spirit can be similar to how you receive salvation from the Lord for your forgiveness of sin and eternal life—you ask and receive. Equally, the Holy Spirit can be received by the laying on of hands by others. We can also spontaneously receive an infilling of the Holy Spirit at the Lord's discretion.

Acts 19:2, 6
"Did you receive the Holy Spirit when you believed?..." "No–we haven't even heard that there is a Holy Spirit"… When Paul placed his hands on them, the Holy Spirit came on them, and they spoke in tongues and prophesied.

The infilling of the Holy Spirit is primarily a work of God, yet there are responsibilities we have in living a life that is Holy Spirit-filled. Again, it is a human-divine cooperative where we see a work of God is contingent upon a person taking initiative on his or her part. As a hot air balloon operator can "stoke the fire" to fill the balloon with more air and make it rise higher, so there are things for which you are responsible for to stoke a spiritual fire that releases more of the Holy Spirit's power in your life:

1. Search your heart and repent of any known sin (Psalm 139:23-24; 2 Chronicles 7:14; Acts 3:19-20; John 1:9).
2. Consecrate yourself afresh totally to the Lord (Romans 12:1).
3. Confess your need and dependence on God.
4. Ask the Lord in faith that He would release a fresh infilling and empowering of God's Spirit to you (Acts 4:29-31).
5. In faith receive and believe that God answered your prayer and walk in it. Thank God for His work in your life.

You don't want to live life in any other way than by being filled with God's Spirit and living in His power. It is only through the Holy Spirit you will live free in a supernatural life, fully engaged in both the heavenly and natural realms!

SECTION THREE
Understanding Power and Authority

Living in God's supernatural power is an amazing right and privilege of every Christian. Jesus promised it. The early Church received and operated in it. In fact, the Apostle Paul said that his life and ministry for Christ were proven "in the Holy Spirit and in sincere love, in truthful speech and in the *power of God*" (2 Corinthians 6:6-7).

The word "power" is an English translation of the Greek term *dunamis*, which means strength, power, or ability.[1] It refers to inherent power residing in a thing by virtue of its nature, and the power for performing miracles. We get our word "dynamite" from this word.

However, there was another key component to Jesus' life and ministry. Luke's gospel account tells of people saying about Him with amazement, "What authority and power this man's words possess! Even evil spirits obey him and flee at his command" (Luke 4:36). Though Jesus was true God, He lived as a man—armed with God's *power*. More than that, He also had God's *authority*.

"Authority" is our English translation of the Greek term *exousia*. It is also sometimes translated "power," but it refers more to the power of authority, right, or privilege. It can refer to the power of government, or the power of a person or agency whose will and commands must be submitted to by others and obeyed.[2]

Throughout His life, Jesus demonstrated both power (*dunamis*) and authority (*exousia*). He resisted every temptation of Satan. He overpowered Satan's kingdom at every front—from healing people to delivering them from demonic assault. Where Jesus showed up, Satan had to flee!

CHRIST'S POWER AND AUTHORITY

CHRIST'S AUTHORITY IS ULTIMATE AUTHORITY

Ephesians 1:19-22
I pray that you will begin to understand the incredible greatness of his power—for us who believe. This is the same mighty power which He brought about in Christ, when He raised Him from the dead, and seated Him at His right hand in the heavenly places, far above all rule and authority and power and dominion, and every name that is named, not only in this age, but also in the one to come. And He put all things in subjection under His feet, and gave Him as head over all things to the church…

- Forty days after Jesus rose—alive—from the grave, He ascended to Heaven. There God honored Him by seating Him at His own right hand, a symbolic gesture of granting power and authority.
- Jesus holds that place of authority even now, but He is not seated in heaven in a far corner of the universe. He is very present in the realm of the invisible.
- Jesus is the ultimate authority over all the spirit beings in the invisible realm—including Satan. Satan is merely a being, created by God.
- No one or no thing has greater power or authority than Jesus. God has placed all things under Jesus' feet.

JESUS MINISTERED UNDER GOD'S AUTHORITY

Jesus' authority was and is greater than all creation and created beings. He ministered in divine power and authority. He also ministered under a context of authority Himself. Jesus never operated outside of God's direction and authority. He did not independently determine what He would do, or how He would do anything. In fact, He did not even say anything unless He heard from His Father that He should speak (John 8:26, 12:49).

Jesus was submissive to God the Father and moved in and under His authority in all He did. It was in this way that He lived "anointed," or empowered, by the Holy Spirit. Jesus, though He was true God as well as being true man, was a man who ministered under the authority of God the Father.

John 5:30
But I do nothing without consulting the Father. I judge as I am told. And My judgment is absolutely just, because it is according to the will of God who sent Me; it is not merely My own.

John 7:16
So Jesus told them, "I'm not teaching my own ideas, but those of God who sent me."

> Jesus was submissive to God the Father and moved in and under His authority in all He did. It was in this way that He lived "anointed," or empowered, by the Holy Spirit.

John 8:26; 28
"I have much to say about you and much to condemn, but I won't. For I say only what I have heard from the one who sent me, and he is true." So Jesus said, "When you have lifted up the Son of Man on the cross, then you will realize that I am He and that I do nothing on my own, but I speak what the Father taught me."

John 12:49-50
I don't speak on my own authority. The Father who sent me gave me his own instructions as to what I should say. And I know His instructions lead to eternal life; so I say whatever the Father tells me to say!

Because Jesus ministered *under* authority He was able to minister *in* great authority. It is critical that we, too, learn to live and operate in the context of authority—submissive to God and to the authority structures He has placed in our lives—so that the power of God can be exercised in and through us, and so that we can live in divine power like Jesus did.

CARRYING OUT JESUS' MINISTRY REQUIRES JESUS' AUTHORITY AND POWER

To truly be "living free"—and to be able to carry out Jesus' ministry on earth the way that both He and the early Church did—requires that we receive and move in God's power and God's authority. As believing followers of Jesus Christ, we will discover that to be who we are to be, to live the way we are to live, and to do what we are to do requires God's supernatural power in our lives.

This is why "He called the twelve together and gave them *power* and *authority* over all the demons, and to heal diseases" (Luke 9:1). This is why when Jesus prepared to return to heaven after His resurrection from death He told His disciples to wait until the Holy Spirit came and filled them with God's power that was from heaven.

Luke 24:49
And now I will send the Holy Spirit, just as My Father promised. But stay here in the city until the Holy Spirit comes and fills you with power from heaven.

Acts 1:8
But when the Holy Spirit has come upon you, you will receive power and will tell people about Me everywhere in Jerusalem, throughout Judea, in Samaria, and to the ends of the earth.

The Scriptures are very clear. God has extended Christ's authority to us, His disciples.

THE DISTINCTION BETWEEN POWER AND AUTHORITY

There is a distinct difference between God's authority and God's power, though they are inseparably interrelated. It was recognized by those who observed Jesus that He operated in both authority and power. Christ gave His disciples authority and power over all demons and disease.

Luke 4:36
All the people were amazed and said to each other, "What is this teaching? With authority and power he gives orders to evil spirits and they come out!"

Luke 9:1
When Jesus had called the Twelve together, he gave them power and authority to drive out all demons and to cure diseases.

1. Authority is the *right* to rule.
2. Power is the *ability* to rule.

Authority

Authority is based upon the position one has, which gives that person the *right* to rule within the limits and the scope of a designated authority. For example, a police officer has authority in a given domain as extended and defined by the governing civil authorities. However, he or she would not have authority to rule over people in other realms. He (or she) could not simply march into a battalion headquarters on a military base and start directing soldiers there.

The Scriptures are very clear. God has extended Christ's authority to us, His disciples, to carry out and extend His business in advancing His kingdom, within the scope and parameters He has established for us.

Power

Power is the capacity a person has to exercise God's authority. Stated another way, the power of God is related to a person's ability to exercise the authority that inherently belongs to every Christian. Whereas authority is absolute due to our position of being united to Jesus Christ in salvation, power exercised in the believer is relative. Sin and strongholds, as we will soon see, can compromise the power of God in a Christian.

For example, the Scriptures point out that such sins and strongholds of unbelief, fear, pride, inferiority, and many more weaken God's power being released in God's people. Even Jesus could not do many works of supernatural power in Nazareth because of their unbelief (Mark 6:6).

JESUS GIVES HIS AUTHORITY TO US

Scripture tells us we used to be under the dominion of hell, Satan, and his minions, governed by our sinful flesh nature and influenced by the world system (see Ephesians 2:1-3). Jesus came and delivered us from the dominion (power and authority) of Satan and transferred us into His kingdom. The amazing capstone to this unbelievable gospel transaction is that Jesus not only delivered us from Satan's domain and placed us in His kingdom, but He swept us up and seated us with Him in the heavenlies! This means the authority given to Jesus by His Father has been given to us!

Ephesians 2:4-6
But because of His great love for us, God, who is rich in mercy, made us alive with Christ even when we were dead in transgressions—it is by grace you have been saved. And God raised us up with Christ and seated us with Him in the heavenly realms in Christ Jesus.

Jesus rules over the entire heavenlies realm, seated in the place of ultimate authority—and we reign with Him and share His authority in the heavenlies realm. This is a present reality, not one that will be realized only in the future. We now possess every spiritual blessing in the heavenlies, through Christ (Ephesians 1:3).

Luke 10:1, 17-19 (NIV)
The Lord now chose seventy-two other disciples and sent them on ahead in pairs to all the towns and villages he planned to visit....And the seventy-two returned with joy, saying, "Lord, even the demons are subject to us in Your name." And He said to them, "I was watching Satan fall from heaven like lightning. "Behold, I have given you authority to tread upon serpents and scorpions, and over all the power of the enemy, and nothing shall injure you."

ALL BELIEVERS RECEIVE JESUS' AUTHORITY

The power and authority Jesus extended to His disciples wasn't just for them—it was for us too. Jesus told the disciples, "The truth is, ANYONE who believes in me will do the same works I have done, and even greater works" (John 14:12, emphasis added). Jesus didn't intend for us to let Him do all the work of declaring and establishing the Kingdom of God on earth. Neither did He intend for that authority and ministry to die with the first-century disciples. He fully intended for ALL His followers to share in His power and authority!

Matthew 28:18
Jesus came and told his disciples, "I have been given complete authority in heaven and on earth. Therefore, go and make disciples of all the nations, baptizing them in the name of the Father and the Son and the Holy Spirit. Teach these new disciples to obey all the

> The authority given to Jesus by His Father has been given to us! Jesus fully intended for ALL His followers to share in His power and authority!

commands I have given you. And be sure of this: I am with you always, even to the end of the age."

John 17:18, 20-21

As you sent me into the world, I am sending them into the world. I am praying not only for these disciples but also for all who will ever believe in me because of their testimony. My prayer for all of them is that they will be one, just as you and I are one, Father—that just as you are in me and I am in you, so they will be in us, and the world will believe you sent me.

Ephesians 1:19-22; 2:6 (NIV)

I pray that you will begin to understand the incredible greatness of his power for us who believe him. This is the same mighty power that raised Christ from the dead and seated him in the place of honor at God's right hand in heavenly realms. Now he is far above any ruler or authority or power or leader or anything else in this world or in the world to come. And God has put all things under the authority of Christ, and he gave him this authority for the benefit of the church. And God raised us up with Christ and seated us with him in the heavenly realms in Christ Jesus.

James 5:17-18 (NIV)

Elijah was a man just like us. He prayed earnestly that it would not rain, and it did not rain on the land for three and a half years. Again he prayed, and the heavens gave rain, and the earth produced its crops.

WE RECEIVE THIS AUTHORITY AT SALVATION

AT SALVATION CHRISTIANS ARE SEATED WITH CHRIST

Jesus rules over all the heavenlies, and is seated in the place of ultimate authority and we reign with Him (Ephesians 1:20-21, 2:6). We share in Jesus' own authority in the heavenlies. We now "proclaim the manifold wisdom of God" to the rulers and authorities in the heavenlies (Ephesians 3:10); that is, we have the right and responsibility to enforce God's authority, much the way a federal agent is deputized by the government to enforce its laws and boundaries.

Colossians 2:9-10

For in Christ all the fullness of the Deity lives in bodily form, and you have been given fullness in Christ, who is the head over every power and authority.

Colossians 2:13-15

When you were dead in your sins and in the uncircumcision of your sinful nature, God made you alive with Christ. He forgave us all our sins, having canceled the written code, with its regulations, that was against us and that stood opposed to us; he took it away, nailing it to the cross. And having disarmed the powers and authorities, he made a public spectacle of them, triumphing over them by the cross.

"Living free" means being set free from the power and authority of Satan and being released to live and operate in the power and authority of God. How is it that we are able to do this? We do it by virtue of our position in—and personal relationship with—Jesus Christ. As believers, we must begin to understand and regularly appropriate the power and authority of Jesus Christ that belongs to and is resident within us.

There is only one way to receive and be able to live in God's authority and power—it is through entering into a redemptive saving relationship with Jesus Christ. Another way of saying this is that receiving salvation from your sin in and through Jesus Christ allows you to enter into His authority.

Have you made the spiritual transaction of receiving Jesus Christ into your life and being forgiven from the sin that separates you from God? Take some time to go back to Section One in this manual and revisit the basic truths there. They can help you understand how to be sure you have a saving relationship with God through Jesus Christ. We can never hear these truths too often!

Unbeliever	Believer
Jesus Christ Ephesians 1:22	**Jesus Christ** Ephesians 1:22
	Believers Ephesians 2:6
Satan Ephesians 2:2	**Satan** Ephesians 2:2
Spirits Luke 13:11	**Spirits** Luke 13:11
Human Beings Genesis 1:26	**Human Beings** Genesis 1:26
Animals Psalms 8:6-8	**Animals** Psalms 8:6-8

This represents the hierarchy of spiritual authority in the world. Note that when a person becomes a Christian, he/she relocates on the authority ladder to just under Jesus Christ.

2 Peter 1:12-15

Therefore, I will always remind you about these things—even though you already know them and are standing firm in the truth you have been taught. And it is only right that I should keep on reminding you as long as I live. For our Lord Jesus Christ has shown me that I must soon leave this earthly life, so I will work hard to make sure you always remember these things after I am gone.

If you prayed in sincere faith to receive the work of Jesus Christ in your life, you can be confident that your spiritual transaction took place. God delights in giving forgiveness and eternal life to mankind.

By virtue of this indwelling presence of Jesus Christ in you, you have a new identity and a new nature. They are divine and supernatural. Everything that is Christ's is imparted to you at salvation.

Romans 10:13 (ESV)

For "everyone who calls on the name of the Lord will be saved."

2 Corinthians 5:17 (ESV)

Therefore, if anyone is in Christ, he is a new creation. The old has passed away; behold, the new has come.

AT SALVATION YOU HAVE THE FULLNESS OF CHRIST

You Are Indwelt by Jesus Christ

The Apostle Paul uses the phrase "in Christ" at least 86 times in His writings. The essence of you becoming a new creation in Christ (2 Corinthians 5:21) is the fact that Christ lives in you. He indwells you by His Spirit. This is not merely a theological concept or mystical symbolism—it is a reality! By virtue of this indwelling presence of Jesus Christ in you, you have a new identity and a new nature. They are divine and supernatural. Everything that is Christ's is imparted to you at salvation.

Galatians 2:20

I have been crucified with Christ and I no longer live, but Christ lives in me. The life I live in the body, I live by faith in the Son of God, who loved me and gave himself for me.

Colossians 1:27

To them God has chosen to make known among the Gentiles the glorious riches of this mystery, which is Christ in you, the hope of glory.

You Are Full in Christ

The Scriptures state that "in Christ" we have every spiritual blessing in the *heavenlies* (Ephesians 1:3). Similarly, they clearly state that the Christian has been given the fullness of God in and through Jesus Christ, just as He has the fullness of God in His bodily form.

Colossians 2:9-10

For in Christ all the fullness of the Deity lives in bodily form, and you have been given fullness in Christ, who is the head over every power and authority.

The English word translated "fullness" is from the Greek word *pleroma*. It means "complete: full, not lacking anything, perfect, whole, finished." Christ in us imparts to us every supernatural resource, blessing, and inheritance we need to live like Him!

Jesus Christ's Glory Is Resident in You

We see God's glory demonstrated many times in the Scriptures. It is revealed in accounts such as at Mt. Sinai when the Israelites witnessed the phenomenal powers of earthquakes and lightning (Exodus 19). We see it likewise when Moses could not withstand the weightiness of God's presence in the tabernacle (Exodus 40), or when the priests could not stand in the temple due to God's manifested glory (2 Chronicles 7:1-2). Isaiah experienced a meltdown when exposed to a portion of God's glory (Isaiah 6). And who could forget the traumatic encounter Peter, James, and John experienced at the mountain when they witnessed Jesus being partially transfigured in His glory (Luke 9). In each account, the people involved were overwhelmed by the manifest (revealed) glory of God.

Amazingly, the Scriptures clearly state that all Christians have this very same glory in our physical bodies. Again, this is not merely a theological concept but a very powerful reality.

2 Corinthians 4:4, 6, 7

The god of this age has blinded the minds of unbelievers, so that they cannot see the light of the gospel of the glory of Christ, who is the image of God. . . . For God, who said, "Let light shine out of darkness," made his light shine in our hearts to give us the light of the knowledge of the glory of God in the face of Christ. . . . But we have this treasure in jars of clay to show that this all-surpassing power is from God and not from us.

You Are Fully Secured in God's Love

God does not just fit us for service like a well-recharged power tool! We are His children, loved and adored. Again, this is because of our union in Jesus Christ. We are loved by God with the same love with which He loves His Son Jesus Christ.

John 17:21-23

…that all of them may be one, Father, just as you are in me and I am in you. May they also be in us so that the world may believe that you have sent me. I have given them the glory that you gave me, that they may be one as we are one: I in them and you in me. May they be brought to complete unity to let the world know that you sent me and have loved them even as you have loved me.

The Apostle Paul knew that our experience of living increasingly in the fullness of God's life and power is connected (and proportionate) to our being secured in God's love.

Ephesians 3:18-20

And may you have the power to understand, as all God's people should, how wide, how long, how high, and how deep his love is. May you experience the love of Christ, though it is too great to understand fully. <u>Then you will be made complete with all the fullness of life and power that comes from God.</u> Now all glory to God, who is able, through his mighty power at work within us, to accomplish infinitely more than we might ask or think (emphasis added).

God cannot love us more than He does today, but we can walk into greater and greater revelation and experience of His love.

AT SALVATION YOU ENTER INTO A WAR

As Christians, when we are raised up and seated positionally with Christ in the heavenlies, we enter into a place of authority and responsibility in a cosmic war—a war between the kingdom of God and the kingdom of Satan. These kingdoms are not equally powerful, we must remember. The war raging in the heavenlies since Lucifer's (now Satan's) rebellion is an insurrection of a lesser power against a greater. God is still ultimately in control.[3]

That being said, there are still spiritual battles raging all around us, which we experience in the natural. To be victorious, and to fulfill God's plan and purpose for us on this earth, we must learn to use our divinely powerful and spiritual weapons, exercise our authority, and do battle in the heavenlies. We need to take back territory the enemy has stolen in people's lives and in the world, and thereby plunder Satan's kingdom on earth. This is what we are on earth to do—to extend Jesus' ministry and kingdom. Jesus' life and ministry is our model for how life is to be lived, and how the Church is to operate today.

- We must use our weapons, exercise our authority, and do battle in the heavenlies.

We are in a war, and we cannot ignore our enemies. God has given us divinely powerful weapons to defeat them (2 Corinthians 10:4).

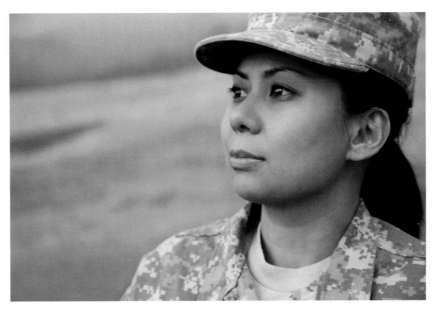

- We have the authority of Christ; the enemy cannot stand up against us in a direct confrontation of authority.

- The weapons available to Satan are lying, working covertly, deceiving, intimidating, and causing fear. He cannot withstand a power encounter against God's children who stand in the righteousness, holiness, and authority of Christ.

The Scriptures, the commission of Jesus Christ, and the times in which we live demand our attention to this aspect of Christian life and ministry. We cannot afford to neglect or marginalize this arena of Christian living.

We are in a war, and we cannot ignore our enemies. God has given us divinely powerful weapons to defeat them (2 Corinthians 10:4). As Jesus did, so must we forcefully rebuke and evict demonic beings in the specific assaults, strongholds, sins, and temptations we encounter in our daily lives.

CONCLUSION

The purpose of this manual is to give you truths for truly "living free." This includes recovering the spiritual authority God originally designed for His people to possess. It includes learning how to effectively and powerfully use the authority God has given you through Jesus Christ, to deal with the assaults and torments that evil spirits will try to bring against you. You CAN rebuke and resist them the way Jesus and the apostles did. Jesus encouraged us with the truth that "greater is He who lives in you (Jesus Christ by the Holy Spirit) than he who is in the world (Satan and his subservient evil spirits)" (1 John 4:4).

You can be confident that if you have received Jesus Christ as your Lord and Savior, your spiritual transaction took place. Positionally, you are seated with Him in the heavenlies—you share His power and authority. You have a relationship with Him whereby you can hear His voice about how and where He wants you to exercise that authority—through His written Word, the Bible, and through His revealed Word to you in times of prayer.

James 4:7 gives a promise that if we "resist" the devil he will flee from us. It does not say that if we "ignore" the devil he will flee!

If you are a believing follower of Jesus Christ, you are a joint-heir with Him. You now have the authority and power of Jesus Christ resident within you. With that in mind, it is now time to begin reclaiming what the enemy has stolen from you, personally. It is time to exercise your God-given authority over the enemy of your soul and continue God's *sozo* work in your life!

EXERCISE YOUR AUTHORITY

Can you identify anything in your life that is not consistent with God's kingdom values, with how He designed life to be lived—fully and abundantly? Often these areas of discouragement, opposition, or inconsistency are simply just schemes or activities of the enemy. They might be temptations, fears, or thoughts about God, yourself, or others that are not consistent with God's truth. They might include unnecessary and relentless sicknesses. They might include your children having nightmares or any other difficult or uncomfortable circumstances with which you have simply made peace, thinking that is just the way life must be.

James 4:7 gives a promise that if we "resist" the devil he will flee from us. It DOES NOT say that if we "ignore" the devil he will flee! Break through any passivity and humanistic rationalism that keeps you locked down from appropriating (and using) the resources God has provided for you. Begin to exercise the authority and power that is yours in Jesus Christ!

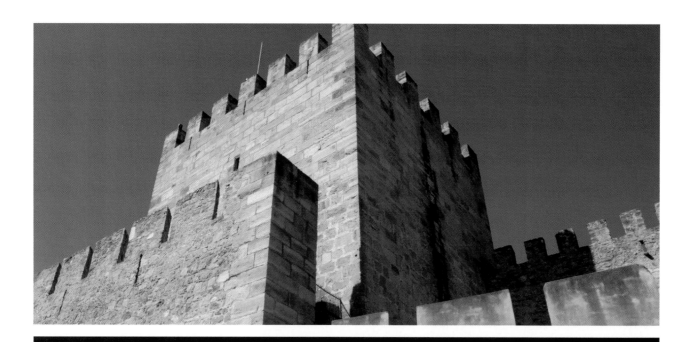

SECTION FOUR
Strongholds and How They Are Built

UNDERSTANDING STRONGHOLDS

As anyone who has been saved longer than five minutes knows, Christians still continue to sin. Which of us cannot relate to the Apostle Paul's anguished struggle?

"I want to do what is right, but I can't. I want to do what is good, but I don't. I don't want to do what is wrong, but I do it anyway. But if I do what I don't want to do, I am not really the one doing wrong; it is sin living in me that does it. I have discovered this principle of life—that when I want to do what is right, I inevitably do what is wrong. I love God's law with all my heart. But there is another power within me that is at war with my mind. This power makes me a slave to the sin that is still within me. Oh, what a miserable person I am! Who will free me from this life that is dominated by sin and death? Thank God! The answer is in Jesus Christ our Lord" (Romans 7:18-25).

So, if faith in Jesus "sets us free," then why do sincere believers who love God continue to struggle with besetting sins, lustful thoughts, pride, depression, fear, anger, and other ungodly attitudes and behaviors? Can believers be held captive to sin in ways that is not instantly resolved when they are saved? Experience tells us—yes!

Paul went on to describe in his letter to the Corinthian Christians just exactly how our minds (and therefore our lives) become captive to sin, and how we can be set free through Jesus Christ:

2 Corinthians 10:3-5 (NKJV)

*For though we walk in the flesh, we do not war according to the flesh. For the weapons of our warfare are not carnal but mighty in God for pulling down **strongholds**, casting down arguments and every high thing that exalts itself against the knowledge of God, bringing every thought into captivity to the obedience of Christ* (emphasis added).

2 Corinthians 10:3-5 (NASB)

For though we walk in the flesh, we do not war according to the flesh, for the weapons of our warfare are not of the flesh, but divinely powerful for the destruction of <u>fortresses</u>. We are destroying speculations and every lofty thing raised up against the knowledge of God, and we are taking every thought captive to the obedience of Christ (emphasis added).

We can be taken captive, Scripture tells us in this passage, by wrong thinking. And we are held there by *strongholds*.

WHAT IS A STRONGHOLD?

Practical Illustration: Carnuntum

*   Scientists using radar have found the heart of a first century Roman military camp. Carnuntum was one of the empire's most strategic strongholds north of the Alps.
*   A computer analysis has revealed an extensive network of restaurants, taverns, baths, and meeting halls. In its heyday at the end of the second century AD, Carnuntum was home to about 50,000 people.

WHAT IS A *SPIRITUAL* STRONGHOLD?
(In reference to 2 Corinthians 10:3-5):

*   "Strongholds" are thoughts, beliefs, philosophies, attitudes, and values that oppose God's truth. This truth can be regarding God, how God regards humans (especially "you"), about Jesus Christ (what He has done for you and how He lives for you), who and what you are, what you possess, how life is to be lived, and/or regarding what truly brings fullness and freedom in life and what results in bondage, ruin, and destruction.
*   Strongholds are powers of reasoning "raised up" against the knowledge of God. They are philosophies, thought systems, and worldviews that arrogantly contradict and defy the person, character, commandments, Word, and love of the Father.
*   They are part of Satan's strategy to deceive individuals, couples, families, churches, communities, cultures, institutions, organizations, and even entire nations into believing and valuing that which is out of alignment with God's truth. Satan has been trying to get us to deny God's truth from the beginning!

Notes: _____

"Strongholds" are thoughts, beliefs, philosophies, attitudes, and values opposing God's truth.

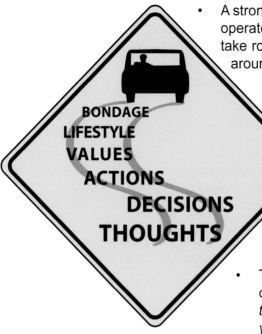

- A stronghold is a **base of operations** out of which Satan's forces operate. It is in such strongholds that Satan's kingdom values to take root and advance in people's lives and in the lives of those around them.

God's Truth Is Absolute

- Every degree to which we are out of alignment to or oppose God's truth—on every issue of life—gives Satan the opportunity to establish his stronghold (or *his base of operations*) in our lives.
- Pride, independence from God, and self-sufficiency are among the characteristics of things raised up against God.
- Truth is more than book knowledge. Truth literally sets the course of our life. Jesus says in John 8:31-32 *"You are truly my disciples if you keep obeying my teachings. And you will know the truth, and the truth will set you free."*

HOW IS A STRONGHOLD BUILT?

Strongholds Are Built by Allowing the Enemy to Have a "Place" or "Opportunity" in our Life Through Sin

The Greek word *topos* is translated "place," "opportunity," or "foothold" in the translations below. It is a word with broad definition which fundamentally includes "territory, land: in the oldest clear use in the singular it means a defined place, then a specific territory, area, or land; district, town, dwelling-place."

Topos carries the idea of "jurisdiction," a legal place in which that enemy can operate. This place of jurisdiction is given to the enemy due to our own sin. or due to a sin response on our part to the sinful actions of others against us (see Ephesians 4:26-27 below). Our mindset is so important as a first line of defense against the schemes of the enemy (1 Peter 5:7).

Ephesians 4:26-27 (NKJV)
"Be angry, and do not sin": do not let the sun go down on your wrath, nor give <u>place</u> to the devil (emphasis added).

Ephesians 4:26-27 (NASB)
BE ANGRY, AND yet DO NOT SIN; do not let the sun go down on your anger, and do not give the devil an <u>opportunity</u> (emphasis added).

Ephesians 4:26-27 (NIV)
"In your anger do not sin": Do not let the sun go down while you are still angry, and do not give the devil a <u>foothold</u> (emphasis added).

THE PROGRESSION OF STRONGHOLDS BEING BUILT

- Even though believing followers of Jesus Christ belong to God, they can give Satan a place or jurisdiction in their lives through unconfessed, unrepentant sin.
- Satan's stronghold construction begins with our thoughts. This is why Paul says that our transformation as believers begins with renewing our mind.

Romans 12:2
Don't copy the behavior and customs of this world, but let God transform you into a new person by changing the way you think. Then you will know what God wants you to do, and you will know how good and pleasing and perfect his will really is.

- It is by your thoughts that you make decisions; your decisions become actions which soon become your values in life. These values begin to define you and then become your lifestyle.
- Eventually, your thoughts and lifestyle can become out of alignment with God's truth. At that point you may find yourself in varying degrees of bondage as Satan builds his stronghold(s) in your life through the place(s) of jurisdiction you gave to him.

THE STUFF OF WHICH STRONGHOLDS ARE MADE

The chart on the next page demonstrates a sampling of Scriptures which show the direct connection between sin and Satan's kingdom. This is not to propose our sinful flesh does not play a role in sin. We, in and of ourselves, have a great enough propensity for sin. When we stand before the Lord answering for how we lived on this earth, there will not be a demonic being next to us at the judgment seat of Christ that will receive the blame for our sin. It is our responsibility and ours alone to bear.

That being said, Satan's kingdom is actively involved in temptation, and in exerting energy against people to draw them into sin. Demonic beings look for any opportunity or jurisdiction in which they can operate their wicked wiles against you! Take a moment to look over the contents of this chart, but also be alert to other Scriptures that demonstrate this truth.

BONDAGE
↑
LIFESTYLE
↑
V A L U E S
↑
ACTIONS
↑
DECISIONS
↑
T H O U G H T S

If you can imagine the above diagram as an iceberg, you can see how behaviors are really just "the tip of the iceberg." They are things we see—the bondages we desire so desperately to be freed from, the besetting sins we long to shake. Where those things are rooted, however, is much deeper, broader, and below the "water line" of our lives. They start with our innermost thoughts.

SCRIPTURE	DEMONIC ACCESS FOR STRONGHOLD
Ephesians 4:26-27 *... do not give the devil an opportunity*	anger
2 Timothy 2:24-26	any opposition to God's truth
Hebrews 2:14-15 *... that through death He might render powerless him who had the power of death, that is the devil; and might deliver those who through fear of death were subject to slavery.* **2 Timothy 1:7** *For God has not given us the spirit of fear, but of power, love, and a sound mind.*	fear
Matthew 16:23	temporal man-centered pursuits
Luke 9:54-56	self-righteous condemnation
Acts 5:3 *But Peter said, "Ananias, why has Satan filled your heart to lie to the Holy Spirit?"*	hypocrisy, greed, lying
James 3:14-15 *But if you have bitter jealousy and selfish ambition in your heart...This wisdom is not that which comes down from above, but is earthly, natural, demonic.*	bitter jealousy, selfish ambition
John 8:43-45	lying
2 Corinthians 2:10-11	unforgiveness
Ephesians 2:1-2	worldliness
1 Corinthians 10:20-21	idolatry
1 Timothy 5:13-15 *And at the same time they also learn to be idle...but also gossips and busybodies...for some have already turned aside to follow Satan.*	idleness, laziness, gossip, busybody
1 Timothy 6:9	covetousness, materialism
1 Timothy 1:19-20	violated conscience
1 Corinthians 5:1-5	sexual immoralities, lack of repentance
2 Timothy 3:5; 2 Corinthians 11:13-15; Acts 5:1-3	false religion(s), religious spirit, pseudo-spirituality, position, recognition

BODY
- Material world consciousness
- Five senses, physical health and appearance

SOUL
- Self-consciousness (inner-person)
- Mind, emotion, and will

SPIRIT
- God-consciousness

UNDERSTANDING HOW HUMANS ARE COMPRISED AND STRONGHOLDS ARE BUILT INTO THEIR LIVES

HUMAN BEINGS ARE THREE-PART BEINGS

Human beings are comprised of three parts—body, soul, and spirit.

1 Thessalonians 5:23 (ESV)
Now may the God of peace himself sanctify you completely, and may your whole <u>spirit</u> and <u>soul</u> and <u>body</u> be kept blameless at the coming of our Lord Jesus Christ (emphasis added).

Hebrews 4:12 (ESV)
For the word of God is living and active, sharper than any two-edged sword, piercing to the <u>division of soul and of spirit</u>, of joints and of marrow, and discerning the thoughts and intentions of the heart (emphasis added).

This distinction is necessary to understand when we consider that demonic beings can interface with human beings. What influence can they have with believers?

The following chart depicts the thee Biblical components of a human being and what characterizes each component:

1. BODY
   - Material world consciousness
   - Five senses, physical health and appearance

2. SOUL
   - Self-consciousness (inner-person)
   - Mind, emotion, and will

3. SPIRIT
   - God-consciousness

The "world" is a system or order by which this world operates. It is seen in the philosophies, values, and worldviews by which people operate. The ordered system of the world is in opposition to God at every front.

HUMANS AND DEMONIC SUSCEPTIBILITY

The human spirit is spiritually dead to God and His stimuli (i.e., His work, His Word, His presence, His voice). However, once a person is born again the human spirit is made alive and secured in Jesus Christ.

Ephesians 2:1, 6 (NASB)
And you were dead in your trespasses and sins, . . . even when we were dead in our transgressions, (He) made us alive together with Christ (by grace you have been saved).

Titus 3:5
He saved us, not because of the righteous things we had done, but because of his mercy. He washed away our sins, giving us a new birth and new life through the Holy Spirit.

The human soul is the priority target for the enemy in establishing strongholds. The mind, emotions, and will are essential territory and comprise the primary arena that the enemy desires to compromise.

The human body is vulnerable to demonic attack and can result in physical sicknesses and disease. There are times when health issues are merely physiological issues due to living in perishable bodies. However, there is much Scriptural and practical evidence that physical sickness can be due to demonic activity.

Understanding the Christian's Three Battlefronts

The three battlefronts are the world, the flesh, and Satan's kingdom.

The world is not merely earth and air, water and space; it is a system or order. Satan is identified as the ruler of this world order or system which in essence is hostile toward God.

The "world" is a system or order by which this world operates. It is seen in the philosophies, values, and worldviews by which people operate. The ordered system of the world is in opposition to God at every front. Such values are seen in the world's entertainment, the world's philosophies of life, motivations, and objectives in how and why life should be lived.

John 12:31 (NKJV)

Now is the judgment of this world; now the ruler of this world will be cast out.

James 4:4 (ESV)

You adulterous people! Do you not know that friendship with the world is enmity with God? Therefore whoever wishes to be a friend of the world makes himself an enemy of God.

The **"flesh"** is the sinful nature of mankind which rebels against God and His ways. Just as the world system opposes God, so does mankind's flesh. The "flesh" rebels against God. Satan uses the world system with its lusts and humanistic pride to provoke us to rebel against God's values and truth through sinful attitudes and actions.

Jesus was committed to relentlessly and powerfully setting people free from demonic activity.

Romans 8:5-7

Those who are dominated by the sinful nature think about sinful things, but those who are controlled by the Holy Spirit think about things that please the Spirit. So letting your sinful nature control your mind leads to death. But letting the Spirit control your mind leads to life and peace. For the sinful nature is always hostile to God. It never did obey God's laws, and it never will.

Galatians 5:16-17

So I say, let the Holy Spirit guide your lives. Then you won't be doing what your sinful nature craves. The sinful nature wants to do evil, which is just the opposite of what the Spirit wants. And the Spirit gives us desires that are the opposite of what the sinful nature desires. These two forces are constantly fighting each other, so you are not free to carry out your good intentions.

"Satan's kingdom" is committed to opposing God and all His creation, including people. Satan's forces desire to tempt, seduce, oppress, and torment God's people. He desires to cause people to blaspheme God through sinful actions, torment them, ruin them, and eventually bring death. Jesus was committed to relentlessly and powerfully setting people free from demonic activity.

Luke 6:17-19

He went down with them and stood on a level place. A large crowd of his disciples was there and a great number of people from all over Judea, from Jerusalem, and from the coast of Tyre and Sidon, who had come to hear him and to be healed of their diseases. Those troubled by evil spirits were cured, and the people all tried to touch him, because power was coming from him and healing them all.

Ephesians 2:1-3 summarizes for us the interfacing of these three battle-fronts in a person's life prior to coming to Christ in salvation:

Ephesians 2:1-3 (ESV)
And you were dead in the trespasses and sins in which you once walked, <u>following the course of this world</u>, <u>following the prince of the power of the air</u>, the spirit that is now at work in the sons of disobe-dience—among whom we all once <u>lived in the passions of our flesh</u>, carrying out the desires of the body and the mind, and were by nature children of wrath, like the rest of mankind (emphasis added).

Paul makes it clear that our fundamental struggle is not against flesh and blood. It is against such evil spirits who will seek to use our flesh and the world system against us in spiritual assault and conflict:

Ephesians 6:12
For we are not fighting against flesh-and-blood enemies, but against evil rulers and authorities of the unseen world, against mighty powers in this dark world, and against evil spirits in the heavenly places.

A Threefold Cord

Imagine this fundamental struggle with the enemy of our souls as a three-strand rope. In order to sever this "rope" that serves to hold us in bondage, Christians must take action against all three and not leave one cord connected:

Cord One: the World

Expose and renounce the lies of the world-system with truth.

Cord Two: the Flesh

Put to death the sinful flesh by exercising truth in your life through obe-dience to God's Word, character, and Spirit.

Cord Three: Satan's Kingdom

Take direct authority over Satan and his demons in order for there to be true victo-ry and breaking free from his strongholds, so that you can truly be "living free."

ROOTS AND FRUIT

The appearance of spiritual strongholds in our lives can sometimes be like bad fruit on a tree–fruit that has strong roots in the very foundational soil of our lives. If we merely try to tackle the obvious surface patterns of behavior in our lives, repenting of those and trying hard to live differently, it is like trimming branches and plucking the away the unwanted "fruit." This "fruit," however, generally just grows back—often quite quickly, despite our best efforts. To get at the fruit once and for all we need to deal with "roots" of that fruit.

This analogy, illustrated below, represents our human efforts to rid ourselves of the besetting sins and ungodly actions and attitudes that prevent us from walking in God's design for our lives, and from moving forward in becoming more like Jesus Christ.

The "roots" of a stronghold (i.e, the causes, not the symptoms) are generally the result of the following kinds of issues in our lives:

- injustices
- love deficits
- trauma
- generational sin patterns
- soul ties
- curses

For now, we will deal with the roots of injustices, trauma, and love deficit sins. (We will more closely examine the roots of generational sin, soul ties, and curses in Section Six of this manual.)

STRONGHOLDS DUE TO INJUSTICES AND TRAUMA

INJUSTICE DEFINED

"Injustice" is best defined as harm or trauma that came in the form of unwarranted rejection, abandonment, and/or suffering. The person affected did nothing to deserve the treatment that was given, and no recourse can be sought. In other words, the circumstances are in the past and can never be changed.

TYPES OF INJUSTICE/TRAUMA

Injustices and trauma, tragically, can take many forms. The following is but a brief list:

- Accidents/injuries/illness/death
- Affairs/divorce/separation
- Abandonment by a parent
- High expectations
- Favoritism towards siblings
- Verbal/emotional/physical/sexual/spiritual abuse
- Drug/alcohol/pornography use in the home
- Harsh, violent, or manipulative discipline
- Response to illness or handicap
- Insecure/unstable home life—moving home/school/city/church
- Discrimination or bullying
- Withholding/being overlooked/conditional love
- Sudden job loss

STRONGHOLDS OF LOVE DEFICIT SINS

DROWNING OUT THE ENEMY'S LIES

God's Unbelievable Love for You

- Satan's primary weapon against you is to make you believe God doesn't love you.
  - The truth of the matter is that God loves you with an infinite, relentless, unconditional love.
  - John 17:21-23 clearly states that God loves His people with the very love with which He loves His son Jesus Christ.
  - Foundational to our living in freedom is deeply recognizing who we are in Jesus Christ, and how God regards us in His great love for us!

Romans 5:8
But God showed His great love for us by sending Christ to die for us while we were still sinners.

Satan's primary weapon against you is to make you believe God doesn't love you. The truth is that God loves you with an infinite, relentless, unconditional love.

Romans 8:35-37

Can anything ever separate us from Christ's love? Does it mean he no longer loves us if we have trouble or calamity, or are persecuted, or are hungry or cold or in danger or threatened with death? (Even the Scriptures say, "For your sake we are killed every day; we are being slaughtered like sheep.") No, despite all these things, overwhelming victory is ours through Christ, who loved us.

WALKING IN GOD'S POWER THROUGH EXPERIENCING HIS LOVE

- In order to fully experience being filled with God's power, you must be able to accept and experience His great love for you.

Ephesians 3:18-21

And I pray that you, being rooted and established in love, may have power, together with all the saints, to grasp how wide and long and high and deep is the love of Christ, and to know this love that surpasses knowledge—that you may be filled to the measure of all the fullness of God. Now to him who is able to do immeasurably more than all we ask or imagine, according to his power that is at work within us, to him be glory in the church and in Christ Jesus throughout all generations, for ever and ever! Amen.

Why would Paul think it so important that we experience this amazing love of Christ? Why did he constantly pray this prayer for the Ephesian Christians? Because love is foundational and fundamental to our personhood:

- God is love.
- We are made in His image.
- God cannot love us more than He does today, but we can walk into greater and greater revelation and experience of His love.
- God sings a song of rejoicing over His people out of His love for each and every one!

Zephaniah 3:17 (NIV)

... He will rejoice over you with singing.

GOD'S OUT-OF-THIS-WORLD LOVE FOR YOU REBUKES THE ENEMY

Ephesians 2:4
But God is so rich in mercy, and He loved us so very much...

Zechariah 3:1-4
Then the angel showed me Jeshua the high priest standing before the angel of the LORD. Satan was there at the angel's right hand, accusing Jeshua of many things. And the LORD said to Satan, "I, the LORD, reject your accusations, Satan. Yes, the LORD, who has chosen Jerusalem, rebukes you. This man is like a burning stick that has been snatched from a fire." Jeshua's clothing was filthy as he stood there before the angel. So the angel said to the others standing there, "Take off his filthy clothes." And turning to Jeshua he said, "See, I have taken away your sins, and now I am giving you these fine new clothes."

HOW LOVE HUMANLY IS IMPARTED

God made us all with a need for a 100 percent "God quality" of love. This kind of love comes from God Himself. The New Testament language (Greek) has four primary words by which love is described biblically:

- *Storge*: a love or appreciation for objects such as flowers, jewelry, sports, pets, or nature

- *Eros*: an erotic, sensual type of "love"

- *Phileo*: is an affectionate friendship kind of love reflective in the term "brotherly love," like that of closest of siblings or best friends

- *Agape*: This love is sourced in God. It lives for the benefit and well being of others; it is the servant of one's will versus being the victim of one's emotion. A partial description of it is found in 1 Corinthians 13.

It is *agape* love that we are speaking of in this section. This love is what establishes our value, worth, significance, and security. God created humans out of—and with the intention of them experiencing—this kind of life. Of course, God's original design for our experience of His agape love was lost at the time of Adam's (and Eve's) sin in the Garden of Eden. However, *agape* love expressed in tangible ways is part of God's original design for mankind:

- Touch—healthy/unhealthy

- Focused Attention
  - Quality time
  - Eye contact
  - Being listened to
  - Doing things together

- Words of blessing
  - spoken into one's gifting/ability
  - spoken into one's being/deepest heart
  - spoken into one's future

KEY WORDS TO DESCRIBE THE SINS THAT RESULT IN UNMET LOVE NEEDS

- **Rejection**: Anything less than 100 percent delight, affirmation, and healthy connectedness
- **Abandonment**: When parents are absent (not necessarily through their own fault)
- **Betrayal**: When parents are faithless and betray trust
- **Withholding**: When parents hold back love or expression of love, often out of their own lack of self-worth and lack of relational skill
- **Abuse**
  - Physical
  - Verbal
  - Emotional
  - Sexual
- **Control**: When parents make too many decisions for their children, including pressuring and/or threatening
- **Smothering**: Overly emotional, needy, and demanding
- **Neglect**: Lack of attention and care
- **Conditional love**: Love and acceptance held back until acceptable behavior (that meets the parents' expectations) is demonstrated

> The responses and coping mechanisms we use to compensate for our love deficits and injustices will influence how we see ourselves and others, and affect our personalities.

- **Performance-based acceptance**: False expectations, parents needing their kids to succeed/perform
- **Dominating**: Using fear and intimidation to control others
- **Shaming**: When parents use guilt, shame, or embarrassment to manipulate children into compliance

SIN RESPONSES TO INJUSTICES AND LOVE DEFICIT/DEPRIVATION

1. When one is deprived of love, the foundation of wholeness and the healthy development of whom God designed us to be are compromised.

   - When love is stripped, one is left with "rejection."
   - Love removed leaves a loss of significance and security.
   - To the degree of love deficit or sense of injustice that people experience in their lives, they will experience a loss of personal value and self-worth.
   - The responses and coping mechanisms we use to compensate for our love deficits and injustices will influence how we see ourselves and others, and affect our personalities.

2. Love deficits and injustices can cultivate sinful responses, and move a person into immature and ungodly ways of thinking and behaving.

   - This is especially significant in the developmental years of life.
   - It develops patterns of illicitly trying to capture that love and significance, and/or self-protection to protect oneself from hurt of rejection, and/or illicitly trying to establish significance and security.

3. The longer people live in "sin responses" to love and truth deprivation in their lives, the more these responses define who they are.

   - It becomes more difficult for them to see the issues because they have developed coping skills to manage the emotional, relational, and spiritual damage in their lives.
   - Many times these "blind spots" can be more readily discerned and identified by others and through revelation of the Holy Spirit (we are usually the last person to see ourselves for who and what we truly are). People will typically or generally respond with sin responses that are prominently *passive* or *aggressive*. While it is never 100 percent one way or the other (more likely a mixture), there will be a dominant emphasis.

Once established, strongholds stop us from fully living out God's original design for our lives.

The chart above demonstrates some of the various sin responses to deficiencies of love and truth in our lives:

Note: The ultimate sin response to the passive side is demonstrated by *suicide*, while the ultimate sin response to the aggressive side is demonstrated by *murder*.

CONCLUSION

Once established, strongholds stop us from fully living out God's original design for our lives. They prevent us from receiving His mercy and grace and extending them to others. They obstruct us from living lives of God's love and power to carry out His Kingdom mission on this earth.

Thankfully, God in His infinite care and wisdom has given us clear direction and divinely powerful weapons to enable us to live free in His truth and agape love. In the next section we will identify and examine the biblical truths that empower us to dismantle strongholds, setting us free to live in the fullness of God's life and power!

SECTION FIVE
Dismantling Strongholds

GETTING TO THE ROOT OF A STRONGHOLD

Strongholds don't appear out of nowhere. As we learned in the last session, the appearance of spiritual strongholds in our lives can sometimes be like bad fruit on a tree–fruit that has strong roots in the very foundational soil of our lives.

If we really want to get rid of the sin issues in our lives—become the person God has created us to be, and be increasingly conformed to the image of Jesus Christ—we need to do more than simply pluck off bad fruit. We need to identify and pull up the entire trunk and the roots of the tree. We will find that once we have dealt spiritually with the roots and trunk, the offending branches and bad fruit will fall away more easily.

WE FIGHT WITH POWERFUL SPIRITUAL WEAPONS

- We live in a world of flesh and blood, but our battle is fundamentally spiritual and must be fought with spiritual weapons.

- We do not wrestle against flesh and blood, but against wicked spirit beings (powers of darkness). The demonic spirits that orchestrate and execute the schemes of Satan are not of the natural world.

Remember:

Ephesians 6:12
For our struggle is not against flesh and blood, but against the rulers, against the powers, against the world forces of this darkness, against the spiritual forces of wickedness in the heavenly places.

IDENTIFYING SPIRITUAL ROOTS

1. INJUSTICES

"Injustice" is harm that came our way in the form of unwarranted rejection, abandonment, and/or suffering. We did nothing to deserve the treatment that was given, and no recourse can be sought. The circumstances are in the past and can never be changed.

2. LOVE DEFICITS

When we do not receive God's quality of love as children, especially from authority figures and parents, we are living in "love deficit" or "love deprivation." The enemy uses these situations and wounds to reinforce the idea that we are fundamentally unloved, unlovable, and unimportant.

3. SIN RESPONSES DUE TO INJUSTICES AND LOVE DEFICITS

If we do not receive significance, security and worth legitimately as God designed us to, from Him and from loving human relationships, then we often seek it illegitimately in sinful (and sometimes self-destructive) ways. When we react in these ways, we provide the enemy a *topos*, or a place to land in our lives and set up a base of operations. These reactions can become so deeply ingrained that they become ways of life. Some people even mistakenly believe they are part of their character.

Sin responses due to injustices and love deficits can include (but are not limited to):

- anger
- fear
- control
- bitterness
- rebellion
- insignificance
- selfish ambition
- victimization
- isolation
- self-hatred
- immorality

We live in a world of flesh and blood, but our battle is fundamentally spiritual and must be fought with spiritual weapons.

APPROPRIATING THE GIFT OF REPENTANCE

The foundational posture for uprooting and destroying strongholds is *repentance*. Repentance is not morbid introspection or ungodly sorrow. Repentance is a wonderful and privileged gift, given by God, which unlocks the door to forgiveness, life, and knowledge of the truth (emphasis added to verses):

Acts 5:29-31 (NKJV)
...God exalted him to his own right hand as Prince and Savior that He might <u>give repentance</u> and forgiveness of sins to Israel.

Acts 11:18 (NKJV)
Well then, <u>God has granted</u> to the Gentiles also the repentance that leads to life.

2 Timothy 2:25 (NASB)
…Those who oppose Him He must gently instruct, in the hope that <u>God will grant</u> them repentance leading them to a knowledge of the truth.

Romans 2:4 (NASB)
Do you think lightly of the riches of His kindness and tolerance and patience, not knowing that the <u>kindness</u> of God leads you to repentance?

UNDERSTANDING TRUE REPENTANCE

- The Greek word translated "repentance" in the previous verses is the word *metanoia*. It literally means "a change of mind." True repentance is filled with radical implications, for it turns us *from* something *toward something different.*

- Repentance transforms one's life, values, attitudes, and actions. True biblical repentance includes a person's entire being: the mind, will, and emotions. This results in new thoughts and beliefs, new words and actions, and eventually new emotions.

James 4:10
When you bow down before the Lord
and admit your dependence on Him,
He will lift you up and give you honor.

- It is *not enough merely to be sorrowful for sin*; one must change his or her values, belief system, and lifestyle in order to make specific changes to turn from the sin. It is important to note that repentance is an ongoing process.
- Scripture is clear that it is dangerous not to replace confessed sin with righteous behavior. The enemy will return to reoccupy the vacuum left by confession that is not accompanied by genuine repentance.

Matthew 12:43-45
"When an evil spirit leaves a person, it goes into the desert, seeking rest but finding none. Then it says, 'I will return to the person I came from.' So it returns and finds its former home empty, swept, and clean. Then the spirit finds seven other spirits more evil than itself, and they all enter the person and live there. And so that person is worse off than before. That will be the experience of this evil generation."

Repentance is not morbid introspection or ungodly sorrow. Repentance is a wonderful and privileged gift, given by God, which unlocks the door to forgiveness, life, and knowledge of the truth.

EXERCISING REPENTANCE

The Scriptures speak of repentance in terms of being a gift granted from God. Yet the word *repentance* often elicits negative—even harsh—reactions. Repentance, unfortunately, is many times neglected, ignored, feared, and misunderstood.

The reality is that repentance is a beautiful gift of God's grace to mankind. It is the threshold by which we can enter into the power and joy of a transformed life. It is the key which unlocks the door to God's treasured destiny for us. It ushers us into restoration and rejuvenation. To embrace (and live in) a state of repentance leads to salvation, life, and freedom.

The Apostle James describes for us the heart condition necessary to experience the life and freedom of repentance in its fullness (see James 4:6-10). It is characterized by humility, submission of heart and life, confession and acts of righteous replacement, and exercising your authority in Christ by active resistance.

This state of repentance is all about the heart:

1. A Heart of Humility

Humble yourself:

James 4:6
He gives us more and more strength to stand against such evil desires. As the Scriptures say, "God sets Himself against the proud, but He shows favor to the humble."

Repentance is a beautiful gift of God's grace to mankind. It is the threshold by which we can enter into the power and joy of a transformed life.

James 4:10
When you bow down before the Lord and admit your dependence on Him, He will lift you up and give you honor.

2. A Heart of Submission

Submit to God:

James 4:7-9 (NIV)
Submit yourselves, then, to God. Come near to God and he will come near to you. Wash your hands, you sinners, and purify your hearts, you double minded. Grieve, mourn and wail…

3. A Heart of Confession and Repentance

Confess sin:

James 4:8b-9 (NIV)
Wash your hands, you sinners, and purify your hearts, you double minded. Grieve, mourn and wail…

4. A Heart of Aggressive Resistance

"Resist the devil." Note in this verse that James does not say *ignore* the devil and he will flee, but instead to *resist* him. Matthew's gospel account tells us that in His wilderness temptation, Jesus rebuked the devil and, as a result, Satan left Him (Matthew 4:10-11).

James 4:7 (NIV)
Submit yourselves, then, to God. Resist the devil…

5. The Promise: He Will Flee

James 4:7 (NIV)
…Resist the devil, and he will flee from you.

EXERCISING CHRIST'S AUTHORITY IN REBUKING THE ENEMY

Repentance, as we emphasized previously, is a *spiritual transaction*. A spiritual transaction takes place any time we speak and declare truth in the authority of Jesus Christ. In your pursuit of freedom, as you take back the ground that the enemy has taken in your life, you can also make a spiritual transaction by *resisting the enemy*. Rebuke him; exercise your authority over him, exhort the Scriptures: God's Word promises that he will flee. Satan fled when Jesus rebuked him, and his demons will flee when you rebuke them too (Luke 10:17, 19; James 4:7).

Jesus demonstrated many times what it looks like to receive and live in God's authority. He showed that He not only had the power of God resident in His life, but also the permission and right to use it. He didn't keep that authority to Himself, though; He also imparted His authority to His 12 disciples and then to 72 other disciples.

Luke 9:1

"He called the twelve together, <u>and gave them power and authority</u> over all the demons, and to heal diseases" (emphasis added).

> *It is not enough merely to be sorrowful for sin; one must change his or her values, belief system, and lifestyle in order to make specific changes to turn from the sin. It is important to note that repentance is an ongoing process.*

Luke 10:17-19

"When the seventy-two disciples returned, they joyfully reported to him, 'Lord, even the demons obey us when we use your name!' 'Yes,' he told them, 'I saw Satan fall from heaven like lightning. Look, <u>I have given you authority over all the power of the enemy</u> and you can walk among snakes and scorpions and crush them. Nothing will injure you" (emphasis added).

It is the responsibility of every disciple of Jesus Christ to live and walk in this truth. We must learn to use our divinely powerful spiritual weapons, exercise our authority, and do battle in the heavenlies to take enemy territory and plunder Satan's kingdom on earth, remembering that:

a. this is what we are here to do—to extend Jesus' ministry and kingdom, beginning in our own lives and spheres of influence.
b. Jesus' life and ministry is our model for how life is to be lived, and for how the Church is to operate today.
c. we need to be prepared to exercise Christ's authority wherever the work of the enemy may show up in our lives and beyond—even when it is most unexpected.

UTLIZING THE "4-R'S"

The following model is just that—it is a model. It is a way to remember and appropriate the truths we have been studying that allow us to move into God's freedom through *spiritual transactions* in a *human-divine* cooperation.

1. **REPENT** & RECEIVE

<u>Repent</u> and <u>receive</u> the Lord's forgiveness. Humbly submit yourself before God in repentance and receive His forgiveness through Christ's death and resurrection. This can include granting and asking for forgiveness.

THE 4 R'S

- Repent & Receive

- Rebuke & Renounce

- Replace & Renew

- Receive & Rejoice

2 Chronicles 7:14
"...if my people, who are called by my name, will humble themselves and pray and seek my face and turn from their wicked ways, then will I hear from heaven and will forgive their sin and will heal their land."

Acts 3:19
"Repent, then, and turn to God, so that your sins may be wiped out, that times of refreshing may come from the Lord."

2. REBUKE & RENOUNCE

<u>Rebuke</u> demonic beings and <u>renounce</u> the lies that contradict God's truth. Resist the demonic beings by rebuking them from the stronghold(s) in your life through the authority and power of the death and resurrection of Jesus Christ. In God's authority, renounce any lies believed about yourself, God, or others.

Matthew 4:10
Jesus said to him, "Away from me, Satan! For it is written: 'Worship the Lord your God, and serve him only.'"

Luke 10:17, 19-20
And the seventy-two returned with joy, saying, "Lord, even the demons are subject to us in Your name." "I have given you authority to trample on snakes and scorpions and to overcome all the power of the enemy; nothing will harm you. However, do not rejoice that the spirits submit to you, but rejoice that your names are written in heaven."

3. REPLACE & RENEW

Confess your commitment to walk in the truth and renew your mind in the truth. Come near to God through washing your hands of sinful behavior, and cleansing your mind of duplicity in your devotion to God. Replace it with obedience and with a single-focused devotion to God. Ask God to renew your heart, mind, emotions, and will through the empowering of the Holy Spirit.

Ephesians 4:22-24
You were taught, with regard to your former way of life, to put off your old self, which is being corrupted by its deceitful desires; to be made new in the attitude of your minds; and to put on the new self, created to be like God in true righteousness and holiness.

4. RECEIVE & REJOICE

Receive the infilling work of God's Spirit. Claim, and receive in faith, the empowering/infilling work of the Holy Spirit to walk in His ways. Rejoice in the abundant grace and peace that is yours in the Holy Spirit!

Titus 3:4-6
But when the kindness and love of God our Savior appeared, He saved us, not because of righteous things we had done, but because of His mercy. He saved us through the washing of rebirth and renewal by the Holy Spirit, whom He poured out on us generously through Jesus Christ our Savior.

FORGIVENESS IS KEY

FORGIVENESS IS A SPIRITUAL TRANSACTION AND A DIVINELY POWERFUL WEAPON

Just as we have been forgiven, we are commanded to forgive. Any unforgiveness we harbor is another access point for the enemy in our lives.

Like repentance, forgiveness is another powerful weapon in the hands of a follower of Jesus. And because it is another example of a "human-divine cooperative"—where we initiate an action to which God responds in a way that only He can do—it is also a *spiritual transaction*. Just as we have been forgiven, we are commanded to forgive. Any unforgiveness we harbor is another access point for the enemy in our lives.

- Just as we repent of our sins, we must forgive others who sin against us.
- We have been forgiven of our debts, so we, too, have the privilege (and responsibility) of releasing others.

Matthew 6:9-15 (NIV)
This, then, is how you should pray: "'Our Father in heaven, hallowed be your name, your kingdom come, your will be done on earth as it is in heaven. Give us today our daily bread. Forgive us our debts, as we also have forgiven our debtors. And lead us not into temptation, but deliver us from the evil one.' For if you forgive men when they sin against you, your heavenly Father will also forgive you. But if you do not forgive men their sins, your Father will not forgive your sins."

Matthew 18: 21, 22 (NIV)
Then Peter came to Jesus and asked, "Lord, how many times shall I forgive my brother when he sins against me? Up to seven times?" Jesus answered, "I tell you, not seven times, but seventy-seven times."

Colossians 3:13 (NIV)
Bear with each other and forgive whatever grievances you may have against one another. Forgive as the Lord forgave you.

UNDERSTANDING FORGIVENESS

Forgiveness releases the flow of God's power and love into our lives. It liberates us. It is so important that Jesus commanded it! As with all of God's commands, our responsibility to forgive those who hurt or offend us is for our own abundance of life and well-being.

Because forgiveness is so very important, it is crucial for us to clarify what it is—and what it is not.

- It is not approving of or justifying the act of injustice.
- It is not saying the offense, injury, or injustice is "okay."
- It is not pretending we were not hurt, wounded, or damaged.

To truly forgive, we must identify the injustice or love deficit for what it truly is. Only then can we legitimately forgive. It is similar to the releasing of a debt, where we total the account owed us then mark it "paid in full." We acknowledge that a violation took place against us, but we are releasing or absolving the offender from paying that debt. This is what Jesus did for us.

What is important at this point is that we turn over this transaction to God. Just as Jesus forgave those who brought injustice against Him and then entrusted Himself to His Father—so must we. He can make good the debt owed against us. We must surrender it to Him.

1 Peter 2:22-23
...who committed no sin, nor was any deceit found in His mouth; and while being reviled, He did not revile in return; while suffering, He uttered no threats, but kept entrusting Himself to Him who judges righteously.

FORGIVENESS IS THE REMEDY FOR BITTERNESS AGAINST INJUSTICE AND LOVE DEFICITS

A fundamental scheme of the enemy against mankind from the beginning has been to generate injustices and love deficits within us, and to trap us in the cycle of sin responses, anger, and unforgiveness (see Genesis 4:7; 2 Corinthians 2:11; Ephesians 4:26-27; 1 Peter 5:8). This cycle can trap any of us. While you may not aggressively retaliate against one toward whom you are holding unforgiveness, you can still be operating in a cycle of offense, resentment, and bitterness. The only remedy: pure and outrageous forgiveness!

1. PAIN & HURT

6. CYCLE REPEATS & DEEPENS

VIOLATION
Active harm or passive neglect; feelings of rejection, betrayal, abandonment, etc.

DEMONIC ACCESS POSSIBLE AT EACH STAGE

2. ANGER
(It's not *right* or *fair*)

3. SELF-PROTECTION
(Withdrawal or hardening; active or passive)

5. DESTRUCTIVE BEHAVIOR
(Overt sin & spiritual, emotional, or mental compromise)

4. LEVELS OF RESENTMENT & BITTERNESS

- You can step in and stop the process at any point in the cycle—but it is easier immediately after there has been a violation or injustice against you, before the wound takes root and bitterness has a chance to sprout (Hebrews 12:15).

- You may have to grant forgiveness in your heart more than once as the wound of the same offense might try to surface repeatedly: don't allow the enemy to gain a foothold.

- Sometimes a particular incident can be so painful that you will need to repeatedly work through it concerning forgiveness. If that is what is required—be relentless!

So how do we start stepping out of our offenses and live in the freedom to forgive? The following diagram illustrates the cycle of unforgiveness, and how at any point a person can abort the cycle through biblical forgiveness:

UNFORGIVENESS CYCLE

5. CYCLE REPEATS & DEEPENS

1. RECEIVED HURT & OFFENSE

4. BEHAVIOR CAUSES OFFENSE

2. UNGODLY REACTION (UNFORGIVENESS)

3. *TOPOS*

BECOMING UNOFFENDABLE

Yes, we CAN become unoffendable—and we break out of the offense cycle through forgiveness. Think of each act of forgiveness as removing a stone from a dammed-up stream. Even the slightest bit of offense or

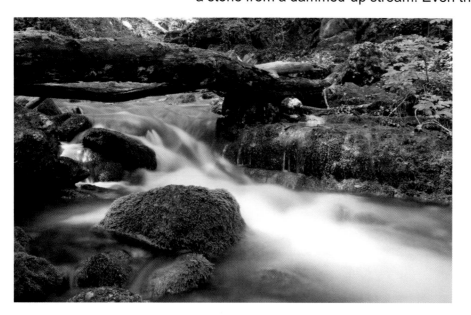

resentment that we nurture grants a place to the devil, in which he places a stone of bitterness or unforgiveness. After a while, those stones fill the streams of our heart and the release of God's Holy Spirit into our life is effectually blocked, inhibiting our ability to relate properly to God and the people around us—even the people we love most.

This was not God's original design for how we are to live. His design for His people, Jesus said, is that "from (our) innermost being will flow rivers of living water" (John 4:14, NIV). Forgiveness takes back the ground that was lost to the enemy through the sin of offense, and restores us to God and others.

Forgiveness is powerful in that it:

- releases heavenly blessings
- breaks destructive spiritual influences
- sets us free to experience God's power in a life of restoration and freedom
- enables deliverance and healing to take place
- is the act of "loosing" (Matthew 18:18)

Forgiveness begins at the volitional level. Extending forgiveness is a transaction of the will and the mind; many times the emotions follow later. But as God deepens His work in our lives, it will eventually affect our feelings and produce acts of forgiveness and blessing. The following diagram illustrates how we can exercise forgiveness, and the life and freedom that follows when we do.

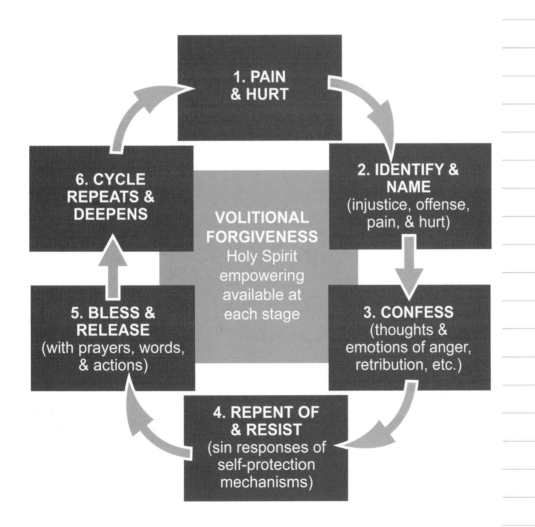

RELEASING UNFORGIVENESS THROUGH PRAYER

The following is a model prayer, not a formula. The point is to genuinely pray from your heart. Here's how you may pray when you begin the process of getting out of the unforgiveness cycle—and begin to live in the freedom of forgiveness!

Dear Heavenly Father, I acknowledge to You today the sin done against me by_____ (name person and the offense before the Lord). What (he or she) did to me was wrong. I choose today to cancel the debt I feel is owed me. I release _____ from my judgment and place him/her into Your hands. I forgive him/her. I bless him/her. I choose not to make him/her pay, seek his/her approval, or rescue him/her from his/her own problems. Please increasingly release the power of Your Holy Spirit to help me transcend this offense and move on in my life in joy and in obedience to You.

I repent of my own anger and bitterness (name any other sin reactions towards the person) and receive Your forgiveness, Lord. I rebuke any evil spirits that would try to take ground in my life and that would energize anger, bitterness, or resentment. I refuse to give them any place in my heart. I command the power of the enemy's influence to stop now and be gone from me, in Jesus' name.

Lord, I ask You to come and heal me, restore and revive me, and flood my soul with Your life and peace. I choose to walk in Your freedom and grace for the days ahead. Amen.

RESTITUTION

Restitution is a very important component of repentance when our sin has brought hurt, injury, offense, or loss to another person. It is often an essential step in the process of breaking free from the enemy's influence (and sometimes outright bondage) in our lives. Many times, without this important step, we continue to hang on to feelings of shame, guilt, and regret which the enemy energizes against us. There can also be hindered relationships between us and the people we've offended until we acknowledge our offense to them, ask them to forgive us, and make right the wrong we committed, to the best of our ability.

Zacchaeus' Offense

In Scripture, we see this concept most vividly illustrated in the life of Zaccheus in Luke 19:1-10. It is interesting to note that Zaccheus' name actually means "righteous." Zaccheus' story does more than demonstrate what restitution looks like; it is an amazing illustration of *original design* realized!

Zaccheus is identified in Luke 19:2 as the "chief tax collector." Tax collectors in Israel in Jesus' day were Jewish men who collected Roman taxes from the Israelites. They were abhorrent to their countrymen, among the most hated people in Jewish society, and not without good reason. Fellow Jews considered them traitors for assisting their Roman masters in oppressing the Israelite people. Besides all that, they were generally corrupt and, more often than not, extracted more taxes than were actually due, with which they lined their own pockets.

Zaccheus' Transformation

Luke 19:8
But Zacchaeus stood up and said to the Lord, "Look, Lord! Here and now I give half of my possessions to the poor, and if I have cheated anybody out of anything, I will pay back four times the amount."

Zacchaeus demonstrated the spiritual transaction that had taken place in his life by his acts of restitution. That which he stole from people he would repay by four times. Then he would take what he had left and give away half of it to the poor. In so doing, Zacchaeus actually went above and beyond what God had required of Israel regarding *restitution*—grace typically goes beyond the law!

Restitution liberates. Restitution has a cleansing effect in your life. Restitution simply is making right wrongs we have committed toward others. We see this clearly set forth by God to Israel in the Old Testament and then by Jesus in His Sermon on the Mount.

> Extending forgiveness is a transaction of the will and the mind; many times the emotions follow later.

Numbers 5:6-7

Give the following instructions to the people of Israel: If any of the people—men or women—betray the Lord by doing wrong to another person, they are guilty. They must confess their sin and make full restitution for what they have done, adding an additional 20 percent and returning it to the person who was wronged.

Matthew 5:23-24

So if you are presenting a sacrifice at the altar in the Temple and you suddenly remember that someone has something against you, leave your sacrifice there at the altar. Go and be reconciled to that person. Then come and offer your sacrifice to God.

Practical Steps to Making Restitution

- Identify whom you have violated and how. Ask the Holy Spirit to reveal this to you, as you may not be immediately conscious of it (see Psalm 139:23-24). You may also wish to ask someone close to you, or your spiritual leaders, to speak into your life regarding possible blind spots on this issue.

- Determine the consequence of your violation toward the person(s). (Ask yourself, *"How have my selfishness, immaturity, attitudes, actions, passivity, or neglect caused hurt, offense, or defilement to this person or these people?"*)

- Determine what the restitution should include and the best way to exercise it. Ask the Holy Spirit to lead you in this. This is not penance or punishment for your sins. It should be a joyful response to the Lord's leading.

- Your restitution will likely include a personal apology and an asking of forgiveness for your actions and/or offenses. It is best to do so in person—at the very least, by phone if a personal visit is not possible. Do not do it in writing, which tends to document the offense rather than removing it.

- Come into the conversation with humility and respect. Do not demand or even expect the other person to forgive you at once. It may take time. And even if he or she doesn't release you from the debt or offense, that is not your responsibility—your part is only to ask forgiveness and make restitution.

Restitution is sometimes a significant part of addressing the roots of strongholds that hold us back in our pursuit of intimacy with God, and living in the freedom of His power and love.

Some acts of restitution might include sensitive issues in which the restitution itself could cause harm or unpleasant consequences. The person whom you violated may not be able or willing to receive your restitution, or even to meet with you personally. It is wise to seek wisdom and direction from spiritual leaders in your life to navigate such situations. But do not let fears keep you from the freedom that awaits you! Restitution is sometimes a significant part of addressing the roots of strongholds that hold us back in our pursuit of intimacy with God, and living in the freedom of His power and love.

CONCLUSION

God has given us, His children who are believing followers of Jesus Christ, all the weapons, authority, and power we need to dismantle spiritual strongholds and live free of the enemy's schemes and bondages.

In review, dismantling and living free of spiritual strongholds includes:
- living a lifestyle of humility and repentance (including the 4-Rs as outlined in this chapter)
- identifying the "roots" of the strongholds in our life and using spiritual weapons and resources (including spiritual transactions made through prayer) to eradicate them instead of merely "plucking the fruit" or dealing with symptoms
- taking direct authority when necessary over demonic spirits that seek to energize the roots of spiritual strongholds and keep us in bondage to their "fruit"
- continuously exercising ourselves to live "unoffendable," being quick to extend and ask forgiveness, and to make restitution for our offenses as the Holy Spirit leads

As you live in this heart condition and posture before God, aggressively rooting out all *topos* or territory of the enemy in your life, you WILL dismantle strongholds and be more and more freed up to receive God's love, and to walk in His original design for you. You will be like the person the Bible describes as a firmly rooted tree, growing strong in the Lord and bearing much fruit for His Kindgom!

Psalm 1:3 NIV
He is like a tree planted by streams of water, which yields its fruit in season and whose leaf does not wither. Whatever he does prospers.

SECTION SIX
Generational Sins, Soul Ties, and Curses

Notes: _____

Sometimes problems may seem to stubbornly resist healing and change, not only because they are spiritually energized by the enemy but also because they are "generational" in nature. Just as a shadow cast by one person can cause darkness to fall on another person, the sins of the generations that preceded us can have spiritual repercussions in our lives today.

The concept of generational sin is difficult for contemporary Western Christians to understand, perhaps because we live in such an individualistic society. Unlike other cultures that are more community oriented, we Westerners find it harder to accept that we bear responsibility for the behavior of others. We tend to deny that our actions can have deep spiritual impact on the people around us. However, there is evidence, both Scriptural and practical, that the spiritual impact of sin can be shared by a family or community and even passed on from generation to generation.

GENERATIONAL STRONGHOLDS

A BIBLICAL FOUNDATION

- The Scriptures are clear that both blessings and curses are passed down from generation to generation.
- This is ultimately seen in the fact that it was through Adam's sin in the garden by which all mankind receive their sin nature.

Romans 5:12 (NIV)

Therefore, just as sin entered the world through one man, and death through sin, and in this way death came to all men, because all sinned.

- Another way of stating it would be that I am living under the shadows of how generations in my family line before me lived. How I live my life can influence and affect the lives of the generations that follow me.

- Generational sins may be part of the reason why some families or communities never seem to be able to break cycles such as poverty, illegitimacy, and crime.

- A generational stronghold may cause a person to be predisposed to certain behaviors or emotions that have no logical explanation in the natural realm, because they come from strongholds that were established in generations past.

- For those of the Western culture this is difficult to comprehend because it works against their individualistic worldview. Yet most of the rest of the world—which tends to be more community oriented—readily lives in light of this reality.

Exodus 20:5-6 (NIV)

You shall not bow down to them or worship them; for I, the LORD your God, am a jealous God, punishing the children for the sin of the fathers to the third and fourth generation of those who hate me, but showing love to a thousand generations of those who love me and keep my commandments.

Psalm 112:1-2 (NIV)

Praise the LORD. Blessed is the man who fears the LORD, who finds great delight in his commands. His children will be mighty in the land; the generation of the upright will be blessed.

John 9:1-2

As Jesus was walking along, he saw a man who had been blind from birth. "Rabbi," his disciples asked him, "why was this man born blind? Was it because of his own sins or his parents' sins?"

Matthew 27:24-25

Pilate saw that he wasn't getting anywhere and that a riot was developing. So he sent for a bowl of water and washed his hands before the crowd, saying, "I am innocent of this man's blood. The responsibility is yours!" And all the people yelled back, "We will take responsibility for his death—we and our children!"

Unlike other cultures that are more community oriented, we Westerners find it harder to accept that we bear responsibility for the behavior of others. We tend to deny that our actions can have deep spiritual impact on the people around us.

There are questions that arise regarding the truths concerning generational strongholds, sin, and curses. The scope of this course is not designed to address such questions. However, these questions are addressed in the book *Living Free: Recovering God's Original Design for Your Life,* published by Sycamore Publications and available through the web page www.sycamorecommission.org.

"Living free" means that we are not living out the sin patterns of the generations that have gone before us. We can break free of the ongoing ramifications of generational sins. In Christ's authority and the power of the Holy Spirit, we can remove the enemy's *topos* or jurisdiction in our lives due to strongholds that were established in our families in the past.

OBSERVATIONS OF YOUR FAMILY LINE

- When people honestly and closely observe their family's generations they will notice patterns from generation to generation, both bad and good.

- The recurring patterns might include besetting sins, strongholds, health issues, patterns of behavior and experience (such as divorce, unwed pregnancies, addictions, abuses), etc.

- Some patterns may run along gender lines.

- Recurring patterns are typically more than coincidence; there is often a spiritual dynamic involved.

How can we know if a sin is generational? There are several possible indicators:

1. **Experience:** The problem stubbornly resists genuine attempts on the individual's part to change. Nothing seems to work long-term, including prayer, counseling, or medical intervention.

2. **Observation and research:** The problem can be seen in other family members in various forms and degrees and in other branches of the family tree. Older family members confirm it has been an issue in past generations.

3. **Discernment:** You have a Holy Spirit sensitivity that "there's more to this than meets the eye." Jesus seemed to rely on such discernment to ascertain that the blind man's infirmity was not generational (John 9:3).

4. **Prophetic revelation:** The Holy Spirit speaks clearly and definitively in prayer, either to you or to another person, that the sin issue is generational in nature. He may or may not reveal the original source. Sometimes the original access point of the sin into the family line is so far back that there is no memory of it in current generations. In this case, revelation has to be acted upon in faith.

> Recurring patterns are typically more than coincidence; there is often a spiritual dynamic involved.

Generational Strongholds

The following is a list (not exhaustive) of symptoms and issues that may be the results of generational sin and strongholds:

- witchcraft/occult
- religious sins
- lying, cheating, stealing
- chemical and behavioral addictions
- sexual immoralities and abuse
- adultery, pornography
- illegitimate pregnancies
- miscarriages and abortions
- infertility and barrenness
- violence, rage, murder
- physical and verbal abuse
- eating disorders
- gambling
- divorces
- suicide
- infirmities
- anxiety, panic attacks
- depression, mental illnesses
- financial instability, poverty, debt

YOUR FAMILY LINE OBSERVATIONS:

1. _____

2. _____

3. _____

4. _____

DISMANTLING GENERATIONAL ISSUES

While Scripture is clear that each person is individually responsible for the guilt of his or her own sin, it also reveals that families and communities bear the spiritual *consequences* of sins committed in their midst. In some cases, when those sins are confessed and repented of by a representative of that family or community, the enemy's jurisdiction (*topos*) is removed.

If you identify that you are living under the shadow of generational strongholds, sins, or curses, you can be encouraged that God has provided a divinely powerful prescription to release you from its hold on your life and that of your family, your church or ministry, your business, etc.

Scripture reveals that families & communities bear the spiritual consequences of sins committed in their midst. God is looking for people who will "stand in the gap" (Ez. 22:30) for their families, churches, and communities.

God is looking for people who will "stand in the gap" (Ezekial 22:30) for their families, churches, and communities. When individuals, in faith, take the responsibility of repentance upon themselves for the sin shadows of previous generations, God honors and blesses those prayers.

Leviticus 26:40-42 (NIV)

But if they will confess their sins and the sins of their fathers—their treachery against me and their hostility toward me...I will remember my covenant with Jacob and my covenant with Isaac and my covenant with Abraham, and I will remember the land.

Nehemiah 1:6; 9:1-2

Let your ear be attentive and your eyes open to hear the prayer your servant is praying before you day and night for your servants, the people of Israel. I confess the sins we Israelites, including myself and my father's house, have committed against you. On the twenty-fourth day of the same month, the Israelites gathered together, fasting and wearing sackcloth and having dust on their heads. Those of Israelite descent had separated themselves from all foreigners. They stood in their places and confessed their sins and the wickedness of their fathers.

Daniel 9:8-11

O LORD, we and our kings, our princes and our fathers are covered with shame because we have sinned against you. The Lord our God is merciful and forgiving, even though we have rebelled against him; we have not obeyed the LORD our God or kept the laws he gave us through his servants the prophets. All Israel has transgressed your law and turned away, refusing to obey you. "Therefore the curses and sworn judgments written in the Law of Moses, the servant of God, have been poured out on us, because we have sinned against you.

Daniel took upon himself the responsibility of repenting for the sins of the nation of Judah. His prayers moved heaven, mobilizing God's mightiest angels to come in response (Daniel. 9:1-19; 10:12-14). Nehemiah, too, took it upon himself to repent of the sins of his family and community in a representative way (Nehemiah. 1:4-7). Eventually, he led the entire community in doing the same (see Nehemiah 9). The city of Jerusalem was rebuilt, and the people's commitment to obey and worship God was restored.

- The effects of sin can be passed on to subsequent generations. Yet, subsequent generations can and must take responsibility for their sin and when they identify with the sin of their ancestors in order to be delivered from the strongholds and curses attached to those sins.

- To break the power of generational sins and strongholds over your life, apply a "4-R" model of prayer but include the generations before you as well as yourself in the prayer. Name the specific sin/ stronghold that you have identified as being generational in nature, renounce it, and cut it off from yourself and your family line.

SOUL-TIES

There are legitimate and healthy "soul-ties" or "soul-bonds" that are part of God's design for life. Some examples of these are spouses to one another, parents and children to one another, church leaders to those within the local church, or spiritual parents and children to one another. But even within legitimate biblical relationships, an inappropriate "soul-tie" or "soul-bond" can develop. This is evidenced when unhealthy, or ungodly by-products of the relationship develop in and through the relationship. These would be seen by some of the stronghold issues that control one's life such as fear, anger, control, shame, illegitimate guilt, self-destruction, etc.

"Living free" means cutting off these invisible but very real and controlling relational cords. When we do, we are able to freely relate to others uninhibited by unhealthy or spiritually energized emotional/spiritual bondages.

UNDERSTANDING SOUL-TIES

- The terms *soul-tie* or *soul-bond* are not found specifically in the Bible but they describe a reality found in Scripture.
- The term describes a relationship that has departed from biblical guidelines in one or more areas. Consequently, an unhealthy relational influence results.
- These often have a spiritual dynamic associated with them that can be influenced by demonic beings—causing an unhealthy, inappropriate, and unbiblical influence on a person.
- The following Scriptures demonstrate this truth. The Genesis account is in regard to Jacob's relationship toward his son Benjamin when Joseph's brothers were negotiating with him for provisions. The Acts account demonstrates how the Apostle Peter was influenced toward distinct errant behavior out of fear of his fellow elders from Jerusalem.

> The term soul tie describes a relationship that has departed from biblical guidelines in one or more areas. Consequently, an unhealthy relational influence results.

Genesis 44:30-31 (NIV)
So now, if the boy is not with us when I go back to your servant my father and if my father, whose life is closely bound up with the boy's life, sees that the boy isn't there, he will die. Your servants will bring the gray head of our father down to the grave in sorrow.

Galatians 2:11-13
But when Peter came to Antioch, I had to oppose him to his face, for what he did was very wrong. When he first arrived, he ate with the Gentile Christians, who were not circumcised. But afterward, when some friends of James came, Peter wouldn't eat with the Gentiles anymore. He was afraid of criticism from these people who insisted on the necessity of circumcision. As a result, other Jewish Christians followed Peter's hypocrisy, and even Barnabas was led astray by their hypocrisy.

FOUR CHARACTERISTICS OF UNHEALTHY SOUL-TIES

1. **Soul-Ties Can Develop Through Sin**

   - Sexual sins: adultery, fornication, homosexuality, and other sexual activity that opposes God's designs according to Scripture
   - Spiritual sins: occult, religious experience dominated relationship, oaths and covenants taken in religious orders, drugs, spiritually cultic organizations

2. **Soul-Ties Can Develop Through Misplaced Trust, Fear, and Need for Approval**

Fear of man = need for man's approval over God's approval.

This becomes dangerous when:
   - we are more dependent upon and/or fearful of a person (or people) and what they think than of God and His appraisal.
   - we are manipulated by the opinion, resources, or pleasure of another person to such a degree that we are not edified and built up into godliness, and/or are not released to walk in God's original design for us.
   - we blindly receive the influence of another person (even if that person is a parent or spouse) without objectively discerning if that person's influence is biblical or godly. (In this case, passivity allows us to be led towards conclusions that are not in alignment with truth.)

3. **Soul-Ties Can Be Caused by Abuses and Violations**

   - These abuses and violations can be spiritual, emotional, mental, sexual, and/or physical.
   - These violations can affect the mind, emotions, and will of a person—which can be the nerve center of spiritual bondage.

90

4. Soul-Ties Do Not Cultivate the Edification of a Person

- Issues surface such as control, manipulation, self-interest, shame, etc.
- Biblically unhealthy relationships cultivate debilitating strongholds.
- "Soul-ties" cause confusion, anxiety, unrest, shame, guilt, and/or oppression.

DISMANTLING SOUL-TIES AND EXPERIENCING FREEDOM

1. Identify the source and cause of the soul-tie

2. Destroy the bondage of the soul-tie

Due to one's own personal sin:

- Confess the personal sin.
- Pray and declare, by the blood and authority of Jesus Christ, a severing of the soul-tie that is the source of bondage. Use the "4-R" prayer model.

Due to being violated:

- Grant forgiveness to the perpetrator, and bless him or her.
- Confess any personal sin responses including any bitterness, resentment, anger, etc.
- Pray and declare, by the blood and authority of Jesus Christ, a severing of the soul-tie that is the source of bondage to the person. Use the 4-R prayer model.

SAMPLE PRAYER:
Lord, I now—in the power and authority of Jesus Christ through His shed blood and resurrection—sever the soul-tie/bondage with _____. I confess myself to be free to live in submission to Your will and ways alone. I command any influence of the enemy to be gone from this relationship, in the name of Jesus, and forbid him from energizing it in any way. I will no longer be dominated by tormenting thoughts, wounded emotions, shame, guilt, control, or fear because of this person. I release _____ from any ungodly tie to me, and I release myself from any ungodly tie to him/her. I forgive and bless _____ and entrust him/her into Your hands. Amen.

How many of us have been blinded to biblical truth due to being numbed by our Western culture worldview?

CURSES

In a newsletter from the relief organization *Food for the Hungry* (dated July 2002), comes the following excerpt from a front page article titled, "Breaking the Spell of Witchcraft:"

Witch-doctors and curses may seem the stuff of Hollywood movies. But unfortunately, for much of the world, belief in the supernatural has power over people's lives.

In Gorongosa, Mozambique, the power of witchcraft is so strong that it is listed as the second leading cause of death. The witch-doctors have even formed an organization that governs their beliefs.

Because witchcraft is an accepted part of the community, fighting demonic powers and the fear caused by the witch-doctors is difficult. Pastors teaching the Word of God are harassed, even threatened with death.

In the Western world, most of us regard curses as part of folklore, fairy tales, and Walt Disney. Often it is the Third World nations who are more likely to give them their due credit. But for our part, we Westerners tend to chalk it up to tradition, lore, and superstition. Believing in curses, we think, is to not be enlightened and sophisticated.

How many of us have been blinded to biblical truth on curses, and are living plagued by them, due to being numbed by our Western culture worldview? Especially among Christians, such a topic is regarded as hocus-pocus, over the edge, purely mystical. Certainly curses cannot be a part of the world of orthodox Christianity! (Or can they?)

UNDERSTANDING CURSES BIBLICALLY AND PRACTICALLY

1. **What does the Bible say concerning curses?**

   - The Bible says much about *curses*—much more than can be addressed in this course.
   - God's Word gives us both a promise and a commandment for dealing with curses. The promise is, "Like a fluttering sparrow or a darting swallow, an undeserved curse does not come to rest" (Proverbs 26:2).
   - Jesus' commandment concerning curses was, "Bless those who curse you, pray for those who mistreat you" (Luke 6:28).

2. Definition (Webster's Dictionary[1])

Curse: *noun*
1. a calling on God or the gods to send evil or injury down on some person or thing.
2. a blasphemous oath; imprecation.
3. a thing cursed.
4. evil or injury that seems to come in answer to a curse.

Curse: *verb*
1. to utter a wish of evil against; to imprecate evil upon, to call injury down on.
2. to afflict; to subject to evil; to blight with a curse; to bring evil or injury on.

3. Description

Primitive people believed that one could pronounce a curse on his enemy and that deity or superhuman beings could be enlisted to execute it. By this means all kinds of disaster, sickness, or hardship could be inflicted. Indeed, the validity of pronounced blessings and the antithesis of cursing in early Bible history is amazing. Noah pronounced a curse on Canaan, and a blessing on Shem and Japheth (Genesis 9:25-27), and subsequent history confirmed his invocations. A curse was characterized as an entity, a power, force, or energy expressing itself in hurt to be feared and shunned. A curse was not considered a mere wish for misfortune on one's enemies, but a potent force capable of translating pronouncements into tangible results.[2]

Proverbs 18:21 (NIV)
The tongue has the power of life and death, and those who love it will eat its fruit.

SOURCES AND ACCESS POINTS OF CURSES

Generational Sin

- The curse could be a result of sinful activity, besetting sin, and/or perhaps occult activity among other things in earlier generations.
- Even words spoken in earlier generations can curse succeeding generations.

2 Samuel 3:28-29

When David heard about it, he declared, "I vow by the Lord that I and my people are innocent of this crime against Abner. Joab and his family are the guilty ones. May his family in every generation be cursed with a man who has open sores or leprosy or who walks on crutches or who dies by the sword or who begs for food!"

2 Samuel 21:1

There was a famine during David's reign that lasted for three years, so David asked the LORD about it. And the LORD said, "The famine has come because Saul and his family are guilty of murdering the Gibeonites."

Joshua 6:26

At that time Joshua invoked this curse: "May the curse of the LORD fall on anyone who tries to rebuild the city of Jericho. At the cost of his firstborn son, he will lay its foundation. At the cost of his youngest son, he will set up its gates."

1 Kings 16:34

It was during his reign that Hiel, a man from Bethel, rebuilt Jericho. When he laid the foundations, his oldest son, Abiram, died. And when he finally completed it by setting up the gates, his youngest son, Segub, died. This all happened according to the message from the LORD concerning Jericho spoken by Joshua son of Nun.

Words that edify, encourage, and strengthen are empowered by God, and are used to pour out His blessing upon people when we invoke His name on them.

Involvement with Unclean or Accursed Objects

- Jurisdiction can be given to the enemy in a family or community through defiling objects and activities.
- Involvement with unclean or accursed objects, most predominantly recognized in demonic idolatry or occult objects, can invoke a curse.

2 Corinthians 6:17 (NIV)
Therefore come out from them and be separate," says the Lord. "Touch no unclean thing, and I will receive you."

Ezekiel 44:23 (NASB)
Moreover, they shall teach My people the difference between the holy and the profane, and cause them to discern between the unclean and the clean.

- These objects need to be identified, renounced, and destroyed in order to remove the enemy's jurisdiction and restore the free flow of God's presence and power in our lives.

Acts 19:18-20
Many of those who believed now came and openly confessed their evil deeds. A number who had practiced sorcery brought their scrolls together and burned them publicly. When they calculated the value of the scrolls, the total came to fifty thousand drachmas. In this way the word of the Lord spread widely and grew in power.

Territorial Violations

- Demonic religious places can be cursed. Sometimes physically removing objects from them, and/or traveling through those locations, can cause problems.

Deuteronomy 7:25-26 (NASB)
The graven images of their gods you are to burn with fire; you shall not covet the silver or the gold that is on them, nor take it for yourselves, or you will be snared by it, for it is an abomination to the Lord your God. You shall not bring an abomination into your house, and like it come under the ban; you shall utterly detest it and you shall utterly abhor it, for it is something banned.

Association with Demonic Rituals or Defiling Activities

- Examples: curses due to involvement with demonic games, music, and rituals. This can include association with Ouija boards, séances, astral projection, psychic readings, demon worship, etc.

Ezekiel 8:9-10 (NASB)
And He said to me, "Go in and see the wicked abominations that they are committing here." So I entered and looked, and behold, every form of creeping things and beasts and detestable things, with all the idols of the house of Israel, were carved on the wall all around.

- Curses on physical locations can also include residual spiritual effects of violations and abuses that occurred in that spot or premises—sinful, hurtful activities that happened there.

Word Curses

- Words can be intentional or unintentional covenants that grant *topos* or jurisdiction to the enemy in our lives.
- Words are powerfully energized by the heavenlies, whether it they are words of blessings or curses.

Proverbs 18:21 (NIV)
The tongue has the power of life and death, and those who love it will eat its fruit.

- The Apostle James described damaging words as curses.

James 3:7-10 (NIV)
No man can tame the tongue. It is a restless evil, full of deadly poison. With the tongue we praise our Lord and Father, and with it we curse men, who have been made in God's likeness. Out of the same mouth come praise and cursing. My brothers, this should not be.

"Word curses" can be self-inflicted curses:

- "I am stupid. . ."
- "I can never be like. . ."
- "I will always be poor . . ."
- Singing lyrics to songs that are words of self-destruction.

"Word curses" can be inflicted on others:

- "You can't do anything right!"
- "Idiot!" (name calling)
- Characterizing people (especially children)—"She's such a klutz, always clumsy," or "He's the shy one."
- Nicknames

Examples of where we might encounter word curses:

- Our own negative self-talk
- Curses from authority figures in our lives (words from parents, teachers, coaches, etc.)
- Curses from others through jealousies, arguments, slanders, and gossip

DISMANTLING CURSES AND EXPERIENCING FREEDOM

1. Dismantle any jurisdiction.

This is done through confession of any sinful activity (use the 4-R's), and/or granting forgiveness toward anyone who has violated or spoken curses against you.

2. Declare your release.

STEP 1: Confess your sin (and any generational sin, if that is the case) that gave the enemy any *topos* and apply the 4-R's to it.

STEP 2: On the basis of His promise of forgiveness for sin, ask God to remove the curse that has been place over your life.

STEP 3: Rebuke any demonic activity and or influence associated with the curse, and command all demonic beings associated with this curse to be gone, in Jesus name.

SAMPLE DECLARATION: *"In the authority of Jesus Christ through His shed blood and resurrection, I take authority over this curse of _____. I declare it has no ground in my life and I command it to be severed and broken **now**!"*

3. Renounce any illegitimate curses.

These can be word curses from other people spoken against your life, either people you know, or those involved in Satan's kingdom in an overt way who may curse you from afar because of your witness for Christ. These word curses are not due to your own sin or activities; therefore, there is no confession of sin involved—simply a renouncing of the curse.

Proverbs 26:2 (NASB)
Like a sparrow in its flitting, like a swallow in its flying, So a curse without cause does not alight.

STEP 1: Speaking out loud, take authority over the curse in Jesus name, and command it to be broken at once.

SAMPLE DECLARATION: *"In the authority of Jesus Christ through His shed blood and resurrection, I take authority over this curse of _____, and command it to be severed and broken **now**!"*

STEP 2: Renounce the curse in Jesus' name, and command all demonic beings associated with the curse to leave you now!

STEP 3: Bless and forgive those who have cursed you.

1 Corinthians 4:12-13 (NIV)
When we are cursed, we bless; when we are persecuted, we endure it; when we are slandered, we answer kindly.

4. **Cleanse your home and life of any defiling objects and/or activities.**

Joshua 24:15 (NIV)
As for me and my house, we will serve the Lord!

5. **Walk in the opposite spirit of cursing—the freedom and power of blessing.**

Romans 12:14 (NIV)
Bless those who persecute you; bless and do not curse.

- As we freely speak and pray blessing over people, God does bless.
- Words that edify, encourage, and strengthen are empowered by God, and used to pour out His blessing upon people when we invoke His name on them.
- When our words are combined with God's Word and character in a verbal blessing, we become a channel through which God's power can flow, much like a lightening rod becomes a conductor for electricity. A lightning rod provides a path for lightning and guides it to the ground in a focused way. In the same way, our words of blessing to others can serve as points of attraction for the power of God to flow into their lives.

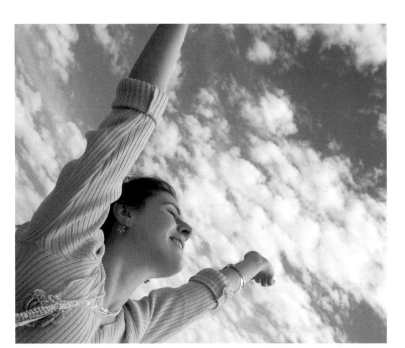

We can take the curses associated with generational sins, soul-ties, and curses—break them—and replace them with God's grace, blessing, power, and love. This is part of the triumph of living free from Satan's schemes to rob you of the amazing design and destiny God had planned for you from the beginning. This is the beauty of living free!

Galatians 5:1
It is for freedom that Christ has set us free. Stand firm, then, and do not let yourselves be burdened again by a yoke of slavery.

INTRODUCTION TO RESOURCE SECTION

In this section you will find resources to help you continue in your pursuit of "living free." Use the thoughts, insights, and Scriptures provided to help you grasp and live out the truth of God's great love and design for you. As your mind is renewed, you'll be transformed!

Romans 12:2 (NIV) *Do not conform any longer to the pattern of this world, but be transformed by the renewing of your mind. Then you will be able to test and approve what God's will is—his good, pleasing and perfect will.*

We've also included six sections on how you can break free of some specific stronghold issues in your life, including:

- Anger
- Fear and Unbelief
- Insignificance and Inferiority
- Passivity
- Rejection
- Shame and Hopelessness

You can use these inventories on your own, with a prayer partner, or with a small group. Allow the Holy Spirit to speak to you through them about ways these stronghold issues have been established in your heart, mind, and life. In some churches offering the "Living Free" course, this can include a session with a trained prayer team to help you pray through some of these things. If this is offered, we encourage you to take advantage of it. You will undoubtedly be blessed and encouraged as you embark on your journey toward "living free" with the help and prayers of brothers and sisters in Christ.

Keep in mind that "freedom" doesn't mean you'll never have to face or deal with any of these issues again. What freedom does mean is that they will no longer have the power to control you.

For a more comprehensive treatment of various stronghold issues and how to pray through them, we recommend you obtain a copy of the *Freedom Resource Manual*, available through Sycamore Publications (order at www.sycamorecommission.org).

ANGER

The Bible tells us that from anger come destruction and ruin—both to ourselves and the people around us. God's design for us, however, is to live free from the control of anger. "A fool gives full vent to his anger," says the writer of Proverbs, "but a wise man keeps himself under control" (Proverbs 29:11).

It may surprise you to discover that anger, in and of itself, is not a primary emotion or stronghold. Anger is a "secondary emotion," meaning other issues lie underneath it to provoke and energize it. These issues can be wounds of injustice, betrayals, abandonments, rejections, resentment, bitterness, and unforgiveness.

Many people live with a low grade of anger that filters everything they see, hear, and say. Some people struggle with outbursts of anger and even rage. Anger is a good diagnostic tool that there is something deeper and larger that needs to be addressed.

Since anger cannot realistically be comprehensively addressed in one sitting, the design of this section is to serve as an introduction. With the tools you'll learn here, you can begin to understand the dynamics of anger (and its related strongholds), and begin to significantly dismantle these strongholds from your life. You'll also gain tools, resources, and insight that will equip you for a life-long pursuit of increased freedom from the related strongholds of anger, injustice, and unforgiveness.

ROOTS OF ANGER

INJUSTICES

Injustice is best defined as unprovoked or unmerited harm that comes our way in the form of rejection and/or suffering. We realize we did nothing to deserve the treatment that we received, and no recourse can be sought. In other words, the circumstances are in the past and can never be changed.

Injustice typically shows itself in buried anger or deep sorrow. We feel justified in hanging onto these feelings, because of the wrongs inflicted upon us. We feel entitled to our anger, sorrow, or bitterness.

Typically, as we move further and further along in the "freedom" process, we are able to see a more complete picture of what occurred in our past. As this understanding emerges, the issue of injustice frequently arises. Freedom comes when partial understanding is replaced with full revelation, and deep, full forgiveness is granted to all who caused suffering or rejected us. We release the past. We relinquish the right to understand. We give up our right to be angry, offended, bitter, or hurt.

Injustices can have a huge influence on our lives. Without knowing it, we can labor under a cloud of perpetual consequences of injustices (real and perceived) in our lives. To truly live free, it is important for each of us to address the a companying tensions and emotions of the injustices we encounter.

UNFORGIVENESS

Unforgiveness many times is directly connected with injustices in our lives. We often live with unhealed wounds as a result of unforgiveness. This produces fruits of bitterness, anger, and rage, and opens the gate for all kinds of enemy strongholds to be built in our lives. Loosed from the bondage that unforgiveness brings, we can begin to heal and the love of God can begin to flow out of our lives toward others.

Forgiveness is necessary when we have been violated in one way or another, through injustice or otherwise. There is a debt to pay before reconciliation or restoration can take place. The debt might be emotional, relational, financial, or physical; the debt might be the result of a betrayal or related to our reputation. Regardless of the situation, a debt is owed to us.

In order to forgive, we must determine that we will release the offenders from their obligation to us.

In order to forgive, we must determine that we will release the offenders (or the offending situation) from their obligation to us. We will not expect the offenders (or the offending situation) to settle the debt or injustice. This is exactly what Jesus did when He released us from having to pay the debt for the sins and violations we committed against Him.

RECOGNIZING ANGER

The following is a worksheet designed to assist you in breaking free from bondages that can be the result of injustices, unforgiveness, and anger. The first section will help you identify how anger might have a place in your life. Mark the boxes that apply:

- ❑ I feel relatively happy, and then I am struck with a sudden mood change.
- ❑ I raise my voice loudly to communicate something that I am emphatic about.
- ❑ I have an expressed impatience with others that oftentimes plays out in exasperation ("Why can't they get a clue?").
- ❑ I often anticipate another person's predictable behavior, and become angry when I see it being fulfilled.
- ❑ I become angry when others cannot "read my mind." I want others to think just like I think and be able to anticipate what I need.
- ❑ I become angry when I am not recognized for my contribution.
- ❑ I become angry when I feel that I am being disrespected or when my words are not taken seriously.
- ❑ I know I am angry because of the language inside my head (cursing myself or others).
- ❑ I know I am angry when I do not want to hear what another person has to say.
- ❑ I get angry when others do not make me a priority.
- ❑ I get angry when I do not have what I need.
- ❑ I get angry when people do not do what I say.
- ❑ I get angry when I cannot control a given situation.
- ❑ I get angry about suggestions that I have done something wrong.
- ❑ I get angry when I feel added pressure on my job, with finances, personal responsibilties, and/or expectations.
- ❑ I easily become defensive about myself and about others.
- ❑ I quickly see the faults in others.
- ❑ I look for opportunities to bring up old hurtful subjects.
- ❑ I find myself speaking negatively or critically of others.
- ❑ The phrase "I don't deserve this" goes through my head frequently.
  - ❑ I say I have forgiven, but I continue to reprocess those subjects in my mind.
    - ❑ I get frustrated easily about the perceived faults and mistakes of others.
    - ❑ I become impatient easily.
    - ❑ I feel like my life is harder than others.
    - ❑ I think, "I have been given a raw deal."

The cure for anger is *forgiveness*. That is why it is important to first understand and experience God's forgiveness of our own sin. God chose to focus on His desire to forgive us rather than hold us accountable for our failures (Psalm 103:12; Isaiah 43:25, 55:7).

The cure for anger is forgiveness.

Unforgiveness demands a payment. When someone has sinned against us and has hurt or offended us, our sense of justice demands that a fair payment be made to us to compensate for their failure. If that person cannot pay—or chooses not to pay—either we resent the injustice and become bitter and angry, or we exercise forgiveness, leading to peace.

Forgiveness is not naturally easy, especially when something has caused us great harm or damage.

However, as we free the offender through forgiveness, we free ourselves from the effects of holding onto destructive attitudes. One barometer indicating whether or not true forgiveness has occurred is our ability through the Holy Spirit to pray a powerful blessing on a person who has hurt us.

RECOGNIZING INJUSTICES AND UNFORGIVENESS

The next section is designed to help you identify ways that you might have received injustices, and/or areas in which there is unforgiveness in your life, starting with your primary family. This inventory is simply a tool to help you to live free from unforgiveness and anger in your life. Ask the Holy Spirit to speak to you before you begin. Ask the Lord, the way David did, to "Search me, O God, and know my heart; try me and know my anxious thoughts; see if there be any hurtful way in me, and lead me in the everlasting way" (Psalm 139:23-24).

BIOLOGICAL FATHER/STEPFATHER

Were the following elements present in your relationship?

- ❑ Exasperation: overuse of, or a faulty form of, discipline that left you crushed in spirit or confused about what you did wrong
- ❑ Control/manipulation
- ❑ Absence of spiritual leadership: Did Dad stand watch over the spiritual condition of the home?
- ❑ Neglect: Did your father spend time with you on a consistent basis?
- ❑ Abandonment: Were you left in front of the TV or in the care of people other than your parents, on a consistent basis?
- ❑ Rejection: Did your parents want you as a child? Were you accepted by your dad? Did you ever feel like you were not the gender or personality your parents desired?
- ❑ Passivity: Did your father lead the home? Did your father initiate? Did he allow your mom to do what the Lord expected of him?
- ❑ Criticism: Was your father critical of you or of your abilities?
- ❑ Performance-based acceptance and love: Were you rewarded with words of encouragement only when you measured up to what your father expected of you?

- ❑ Alcohol abuse
- ❑ Drug use
- ❑ Pornography
- ❑ Adultery
- ❑ Divorce
- ❑ Physical abuse
- ❑ Emotional abuse
- ❑ Sexual abuse

The following areas of omission are things that your father did not do. Often these sins are just as, or more, damaging than sins he may have actually committed.

- ❑ Withholding affection
- ❑ Withholding blessing
- ❑ Withholding words of encouragement
- ❑ Withholding discipline

These areas may also lead to a great deal of hurt and bitterness:

- ❑ Were your brothers or sisters treated in a way that left you bitter?
- ❑ Was your mother treated by your father in a way that left you bitter?

If you checked any items on the preceding list, they need to be brought to the cross of Jesus and left there. For the sake of simplicity, we've provided a sample prayer to help you do that. It is helpful to have someone pray with you and support you as you do. James 5:16 tells us that as we confess our sins to one another we will be healed.

Lord God, I forgive my father (or stepfather) for the sin of _____. (List here all of the sins for which you need to forgive your father. Go through them all one at a time.) I ask you to forgive me for the sin of unforgiveness toward my father for these sins. Forgive me for bitterness, resentment, and anger toward my father. I ask your forgiveness for rebellion toward my dad. I now break all curses, negative thoughts, or slander I have spoken against him. I replace those curses now with mighty blessings!

Lord God, I now want to pray a blessing on my father. (Pray forcefully, with all of your heart and strength; raise your voice, even, and pray with faith.) *I pray that You would:*

- *bless him with salvation*
- *bless him with the same freedom I have found today*
- *bless him with a new and soft heart*
- *bless his marriage*
- *bless his finances and his work*
- *bless him with joy, peace, kindness, love, and all of the fruits of the Spirit*
- *bless him that he will be free of condemnation and shame, and that his wounds would be healed*

- *bless him with a long life and great health*
- *bless him with freedom from all of the schemes and plans of Satan*

I declare that I love my father. I look at him through Your eyes, and see his hurt and his pain. I ask in faith that You would pour Your fire on him. Do it now, Lord! My chains are broken and I stand free before You. Thank You for the power of the Cross.

(Note: If your father has passed away, ask that God would bless his memory and the fruit of his life.)

Pray the following prayer with conviction, with all of your heart, and with faith that God will move in a powerful way right now.

Father, I now renounce a life of anger, bitterness, and unforgiveness. I renounce the right to take offense. I give up my right to see justice. I give You this relationship with my father, and declare that it is in Your hands now. I am not responsible for things that only You can do. I cut that cord now! I rebuke the spirits of:

- *rejection*
- *anger*
- *unforgiveness*
- *abandonment*
- *bitterness*
- *division*

When thoughts of bitterness occur again, rebuke them and stand firm on not going back to take offense. If possible, write a short letter to tell your father you love him, and write out an honest blessing toward him. Do not criticize him in this letter, but simply bless him and let the results rest in the Lord's hands. Even if your father has passed away, there is still powerful spiritual benefit in writing out a release of your forgiveness.

BIOLOGICAL MOTHER/STEPMOTHER

Were the following elements present in your relationship?

- ❑ Exasperation: overuse of, or a faulty form of, discipline that left you crushed in spirit or confused about what you did wrong
- ❑ Control/manipulation
- ❑ Absence of spiritual leadership: Did your mother stand watch over the spiritual condition of the home?
- ❑ Neglect: Did your mother spend time with you on a consistent basis?
- ❑ Abandonment: Were you left in front of the TV, or left in the care of people other than your parents, on a consistent basis?
- ❑ Rejection: Did your parents want you as a child? Were you accepted by your mother?

- ❑ Passivity: Did your mother lead the home? Did your mother initiate? Did she allow your father to do what the Lord expected of *her*?
- ❑ Criticism: Was your mother critical of you or of your abilities?
- ❑ Performance-based acceptance and love: were you rewarded with words of encouragement only when you measured up to what your mother expected of you?
- ❑ Alcohol abuse
- ❑ Drug use
- ❑ Adultery
- ❑ Divorce
- ❑ Physical abuse
- ❑ Emotional abuse
- ❑ Sexual abuse

The following areas of omission are things that your mother did not do. Often these sins are more damaging than sins she may have actually committed.

- ❑ Withholding affection
- ❑ Withholding blessing
- ❑ Withholding words of encouragement
- ❑ Withholding discipline

These areas may lead to a great deal of hurt and bitterness:

- ❑ Were your brothers or sisters treated in a way that left you bitter?
- ❑ Was your father treated by your mother in a way that left you bitter?

If you checked any items on the preceding list, they need to be brought to the cross of Jesus and left there. For the sake of simplicity, we've provided a sample prayer to help you do that. It is helpful to have someone pray with you and support you as you do. James 5:16 tells us that as we confess our sins to one another we will be healed.

Lord God, I forgive my mother (or stepmom) for the sin of _____. (List here all of the sins for which you need to forgive your mother and go through them all one at a time.) Lord, I ask You to forgive me for the sin of unforgiveness toward my mother for these sins. Forgive me for bitterness, resentment, and anger toward my mother. I ask Your forgiveness for rebellion toward my mother, and I now break all curses, negative thoughts, or slander I have spoken against her. I replace those curses now with mighty blessings!

Father, I now want to pray a blessing on my mother. (Pray forcefully, with all of your heart and strength; raise your voice, and pray with faith.) *I pray that You would:*

- *bless her with salvation*
- *bless her with the same freedom I have found today*
- *bless her with a new and soft heart*
- *bless her marriage*

Notes:

- bless her finances and her work
- bless her with joy, peace, kindness, love, and all of the fruits of the Spirit
- bless her that she will be free of condemnation, shame, and that her wounds would be healed
- bless her with a long life and with great health
- bless her with freedom from all of the schemes and plans of Satan

I declare that I love my mother. I look at her through Your eyes, and see her hurt and her pain. I ask in faith that You would pour Your fire on her. Do it now, Lord! My chains are broken and I stand free before You. Thank You for the power of the Cross.

(Note: If your mother has passed away, ask that God would bless her memory and the fruit of her life.)

Pray the following prayer with conviction, with all of your heart and with faith that God will move in a powerful way right now.

Father, I now renounce a life of anger, bitterness, and unforgiveness. I renounce the right to take offense. I give up my right to see justice. I give you this relationship with my mother. It is in your hands now. I am not responsible for things that only You can do. I cut that cord now! I rebuke the spirits of:

- *rejection*
- *anger*
- *unforgiveness*
- *abandonment*
- *bitterness*
- *division*

When thoughts of bitterness occur again, rebuke them and stand firm on not going back to take offense. If possible, write a short letter to tell your mom you love her, and write out an honest blessing toward her. Do not criticize her in this letter, but simply bless her and let the results rest in the Lord's hands. Even if your mother has passed away, there is still powerful spiritual benefit in writing out a release of your forgiveness.

HUSBAND OR WIFE, EX-HUSBAND OR EX-WIFE, BOYFRIEND, OR GIRLFRIEND

Have the following elements been involved in your present relationship or in past relationships? These are sins of commission:

- ❑ Unfaithfulness or betrayal
- ❑ Control/manipulation
- ❑ Absence of spiritual leadership: Does/did your husband stand watch over the spiritual condition of the home?
- ❑ Neglect
- ❑ Abandonment

Many people live with a low grade of anger that filters everything they see, hear, and say. Some people struggle with outbursts of anger and even rage. Anger is a good diagnostic tool that there is something deeper and larger needing to be addressed.

❑ Rejection
❑ Passivity
❑ Criticism
❑ Performance-based acceptance and love
❑ Lying
❑ Alcohol abuse
❑ Drug use
❑ Pornography
❑ Adultery
❑ Divorce
❑ Physical abuse
❑ Emotional abuse
❑ Sexual abuse

The following sins of omission are things that your husband or wife does not or did not do. Often these sins are more damaging than sins of commission:

❑ Withholding affection
❑ Withholding blessing
❑ Withholding words of encouragement

If you checked any items on the preceding list, they need to be brought to the cross of Jesus and left there. For the sake of simplicity, we've provided a sample prayer to help you do that. It is helpful to have someone pray with you and support you as you do. James 5:16 tells us that as we confess our sins to one another we will be healed.

Lord God, I forgive my husband/wife for the sin of _____. (List here all of the sins for which you need to forgive your husband or wife, and go through them all one at a time.) *I ask You to forgive me for the sin of unforgiveness toward my husband/wife for these sins. Forgive me for bitterness, resentment, and anger toward my husband/wife. I ask Your forgiveness for rebellion toward my husband/wife. I now break all curses, negative thoughts, or slander I have spoken against him/her. I replace those curses now with mighty blessings!*

Father, I now want to pray a blessing on my husband/wife. (Stand up to pray this prayer. Pray forcefully, with all of your heart and strength; raise your voice, and pray with faith.) *I pray that You would:*

- *bless him/her with salvation*
- *bless him/her with the same freedom I have found today*
- *bless him/her with a new and soft heart*
- *bless his/her marriage*
- *bless his/her finances and his/her work*
- *bless him/her with joy, peace, kindness, love, and all of the fruits of the Spirit*
- *bless him/her that he/she will be free of condemnation, shame, and that his/her wounds would be healed*

108

- *bless him/her with a long life and with great health*
- *bless him/her with freedom from all of the schemes and plans of Satan*

I declare that I love my husband/wife. I look at him/her through Your eyes, and see his/her hurt and his/her pain. I ask in faith that You would pour Your fire on him/her. Do it now, Lord! My chains are broken and I stand free before You. Thank You for the power of the Cross.

Pray the following prayer with conviction, with all of your heart and with faith that God will move in a powerful way right now.

Father, I renounce anger, bitterness, and unforgiveness in my life. I renounce the right to take offense. I give up my right to see justice. I give You this relationship with my husband/wife, and it is in Your hands now. I am not responsible for things that only You can do. I cut that cord now! I rebuke the spirits of:

- *rejection*
- *anger*
- *unforgiveness*
- *abandonment*
- *bitterness*
- *division*

When thoughts of bitterness occur again, rebuke them and stand firm on not going back to take offense. If possible, write a short letter to tell your husband or wife telling him/her you love him/her, and write out an honest blessing toward him/her. Do not criticize him/her in this letter, but simply bless him/her and let the results rest in the Lord's hands.

BREAKING FREE OF ANGER

1. **Repent** of the ways that anger, injustice, and unforgiveness have marked your life. Use the checklists on the previous pages to highlight these, and to help you as you confess them to the Lord.

2. **Rebuke** the enemy for his lies and his influence. Take authority over his schemes to deceive you with offenses and entitlements and keep you imprisoned behind walls of anger and resentment.

3. **Replace** anger with forgiveness. Continually renew your mind by spending time in God's Word, in His presence through prayer and worship, and in the fellowship of your family, friends, and church.

4. **Receive** God's gracious forgiveness, and a fresh filling of His Holy Spirit. Ask Him to give you a new and very personal revelation of His great love and forgiveness for you.

Notes:

LIVING FREE OF ANGER

Affirm the following declarations:

- I will forgive others just like God has forgiven me.

- I will choose to confront issues, to offer forgiveness to the perpetrator(s), and leave the rest to God.

- I will live in a way that offers forgiveness to others.

- I will grow more and more in understanding that the hurts of my past never escaped the eyes of the Lord.

- I will not let Satan keep me in the bondage of unforgiveness.

- I will forgive others regardless of their response to me.

- I will allow others to see God's grace, mercy, and forgiveness at work in me.

- I will know and understand that forgiveness brings freedom and release from my past and present hurts.

Take the following steps in your life to truly start living free of anger:

- Ask God to reveal to your mind the people against whom you are holding feelings that are not right. Make a list of the names as God reveals them; bind any activity of the enemy that would stimulate morbid introspection. Also, check yourself to see if you

Ephesians 4:26-27 (ESV)
Be angry and do not sin; do not let the sun go down on your anger, and give no opportunity to the devil.

are holding any bitterness toward God or yourself and include these names on your list, if this is the case.

- If, after forgiving a person for a major offense, you recall specific, maybe smaller hurtful incidents, don't let your feelings smolder anew. Instead, release the specific incident(s) and hurt(s) to God then and there.

- Tell God you are willing to live with the ongoing consequence(s) of an offender's action(s), and share these with Him in prayer. In faith and your authority in Christ, take back the ground you have given to Satan through unforgiveness. Claim that which is rightfully yours and that Satan has stolen from you through unforgiveness.

- If some subsequent action of a person you have forgiven triggers painful memories and you are tempted to pick up past bitterness, release this temptation to God on the spot.

SCRIPTURES TO LIVE BY

Proverbs 19:11 (ESV)
Good sense makes one slow to anger, and it is his glory to overlook an offense.

Proverbs 29:22 (ESV)
A man of wrath stirs up strife, and one given to anger causes much transgression.

Ecclesiastes 7:8-9 (ESV)
Better is the end of a thing than its beginning, and the patient in spirit is better than the proud in spirit. Be not quick in your spirit to become angry, for anger lodges in the bosom of fools.

Ephesians 4:26-27 (ESV)
Be angry and do not sin; do not let the sun go down on your anger, and give no opportunity to the devil.

Notes:

FEAR AND UNBELIEF

Most of us do not realize how deeply fear is rooted in our everyday life. We literally live in a culture of fear: fear of terrorism, fear of crime, fear of cancer and disease, fear of abandonment and rejection, fear of financial ruin, and more. Fear leads to unbelief in the Word, character, and power of God.

The nature of fear is to deceive (mislead by a false appearance or statement; outwit, misrepresent, dupe, misinform, misdirect). When we are fearful, we are vulnerable to exploitation, manipulation, deception, and control. The enemy knows this and uses it to his full advantage.

The Scriptures make it very clear that the Lord wants us to be free of fear. Freedom from fear is gained as we:

- allow the power of the Holy Spirit to uncover the presence of fear in our life
- bring fears to the Cross through forgiveness and affirmation of the truth
- allow God to encourage and strengthen us in our weaknesses by His power and presence
- commit to take action to move in full faith and confidence in God, His character, His voice, and His Word

ROOTS OF FEAR

Fear is not from God.

2 Timothy 1:7
For God did not give us a spirit of timidity [fear], but a spirit of power, of love and of self-discipline.

- Fear is a result of not knowing and/or understanding God's character and Word.
- Fear is a result of a lack of faith.

Matthew 14:30-31
But when he saw the wind, he was afraid and beginning to sink, cried out, "Lord save me!" Immediately Jesus reached out his hand and caught him. "You of little faith," he said. "Why did you doubt?"

RECOGNIZING FEAR

FEAR OF PUNISHMENT: LITTLE PEACE, HOPE, FAITH, OR JOY

1 John 4:18
There is no fear in love; but perfect love casts out fear, because fear involves torment.

- quiet times and prayer times motivated by fear
- performance-based relationship with Jesus
- fear of failing the Lord
- fear of punishment from God

Forms of punishment we may fear:

- that the Lord will withhold spiritual gifts
- that we will lack deep intimacy with Jesus
- suffering
- that God will withhold Himself, ignore us, not listen (as though we must earn His attention as with earthly relationships)
- that God will be angry with us or will not forgive us

FEAR OF MAN (INSECURITY)

Proverbs 29:25
Fear of man will prove to be a snare, but whoever trusts in the Lord is kept safe.

Isaiah 51:7
Hear me, you who know what is right, you people who have My law in your hearts: do not fear the reproach of men or be terrified by their insults.

- fear of what other people think about me
- fear (imagined) of what others say about me
- fear of being rejected by those close to me
- fear of people in authority
- fear of communication
- fear of inadequacy and unfavorable comparison with others (a comparative person is fearful because he does not believe God has made him for deep purpose)
- fear of confrontation
- fear of the opinions of others about me
- fear of accountability

Notes: _____

Notes: _____

_____

_____

_____

_____

_____

_____

_____

_____

_____

_____

_____

_____

_____

_____

_____

_____

_____

_____

_____

_____

_____

_____

_____

_____

_____

_____

_____

_____

FEAR OF UNCERTAINTY

Deuteronomy 28:66

You will live in constant suspense, filled with dread both night and day, never sure of your life. In the morning you will say, "If only it were evening!" And in the evening, "If only it were morning!" Because of the terror that will fill your hearts and the sights that your eyes will see.

- fear of not knowing God's will or missing the call of God
- fear that God cannot be trusted to accomplish His purposes through me
- fear of being inadequate to respond to God's call
- fear that committing myself to something right now may cause me to miss something better
- fear that committed involvement in a ministry may cause me to miss out on other opportunities
- fear of committed involvement in a prayer ministry
- fear of committed attendance to church
- fear of tithing to the church
- fear that God will ask too much
- fear of praying out loud and being judged by others for how I pray

FEAR OF NEW TESTAMENT LIVING AND THE SUPERNATURAL WORK OF GOD

Luke 8:37

Then all the people of the region of the Gerasenes asked Jesus to leave them, because they were overcome with fear. So He got into the boat and left.

- fear of deliverance
- fear of the reality of demons
- fear of healing
- fear of persecuion
- fear of being regarded as off balance or fanatical
- fear of the cost of following Christ
- fear of the work of the Holy Spirit
- fear of false manifestations
- fear of spiritual warfare
- fear that what is seen in the spirit will not become visible in the physical
- fear of other elements/repercussions of the ministry of Jesus

FEAR OF FAILURE

Fear can work against our faith, sometimes helping to bring about the failure we fear by becoming a self-fulfilling prophecy, of sorts. In Scripture, we often read accounts of people who were instructed by God or His agents, "Don't be afraid!" We are not to fear anything, not even our own failures.

- fear of falling back into sins
- fear that we will not be freed from habitual sins or addictions
- fear of not getting married
- fear of failing in marriage
- fear of divorce
- fear of intimacy and being seen for who we really are
- fear that our children will not "turn out"
- fear of not succeeding in a good career
- fear of temptation
- fear of disappointing our parents or others we respect

FEAR OF BAD NEWS OR CIRCUMSTANCES

Psalm 112:7-8

Surely he will never be shaken; a righteous man will be remembered forever. He will have no fear of bad news; his heart is steadfast, trusting in the Lord. His heart is secure, he will have no fear; in the end he will look in triumph on his foes.

- fear of reports of division
- fear of reports of sin
- fear of numbers being down in our church, ministry, or business
- fear of bad news
- fear of circumstances being hard
- fear of anti-Christian groups rising up
- fearing that family members will be injured or killed
- fear of a sudden downturn in our financial situation
- fearing the "worst case scenario," even when nothing bad has actually happened

FEAR OF OUR PAST BECOMING KNOWN (AND THE POSSIBLE RAMIFICATIONS)

Isaiah 54:4

Do not be afraid; you will not suffer shame. Do not fear disgrace; you will not be humiliated. You will forget the shame of your youth and remember no more the reproach of your widowhood.

- fear of having to tell our spouse of past sexual sins
- fear of suffering shame from our past
- fear that our past may disgrace us, or hinder or stop God's work in our life
- fear of God's punishment for our past
- fear of God's punishment for sins with which we currently struggle
- fear of struggling with homosexuality and what others may think if we confess that struggle

- fear of shame and guilt for having had an abortion
- fear that we may not be healed from scars or wounds (including sexually-transmitted diseases) that occurred in our past
- fear of being found out for "who we really are"

SUDDEN, UNNATURAL FEARS (WHICH ARE ALWAYS FROM SATAN)

Proverbs 3:24-25
When you lie down, you will not be afraid; when you lie down, your sleep will be sweet. Have no fear of sudden disaster or of the ruin that overtakes the wicked.

- fear of loneliness
- hopelessness
- oppressive fears
- fear of death
- fear of sickness
- fear of cancer
- fear of spouse, children, or family members dying
- fear of lack of provision (having to go without)
- fear of crime and/or terrorism
- fear of accidents

RECOGNIZING UNBELIEF

Unbelief seems harmless enough to most Christians. It's just an innocent flaw—isn't it? We consider it more a matter of practicality, caution, or prudence. In fact, unbelief fearfully, stubbornly, or rebelliously doubts the Word, the work, and the character of God, and it expresses those doubts in both word and action. It asserts that we have a better gauge on reality than He does. It gives preeminence to our own assumptions, presuppositions, prejudices, and fears.

Consider some of the characteristics of unbelief:

- makes up its own mind about what God can and can't do, what He will or won't do, and how He does or doesn't operate

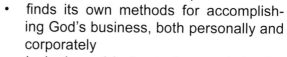

- finds its own methods for accomplishing God's business, both personally and corporately
- looks inward instead of upward. As Jim Cymbala writes in *Fresh Faith*, "Unbelief talks to itself instead of talking to God."[1]

Rather than seeking the Lord and acting in faith according to His character and promises, we depend on our own understanding, our own methods, and our own strength for life and ministry. This tendency toward unbelief often is rooted in fear, pride, rebellion, or other sin areas:

- When motivated by fear, unbelief may manifest itself in self-protective coping mechanisms, similar to those encountered when dealing with insecurity and inferiority.
- When stemming from pride or rebellion, unbelief can be masked as realism, intellectualism, or practicality.
- In the church, unbelief is often cloaked in a critical, religious spirit, as in the case of the Pharisees in Jesus' day.

Even though it may be deeply hidden, unbelief never goes unseen or unnoticed. The Scriptures make it clear that God counts unbelief as a grave sin, and He deals with it forcefully. Large faith believes God—and acts accordingly! Large faith renders nothing impossible with God, and has the potential to move mountains, Jesus said. Without it, as we are reminded in Hebrews 11:6, it is absolutely impossible to please God.

Unbelief seems harmless enough to most Christians. In fact, unbelief fearfully, stubbornly, or rebelliously doubts the Word, the work, and the character of God.

FRUITS OF UNBELIEF

- obstructs God's presence and power in our lives
- opens the door to taking offense, especially toward God and many times toward those who are living in obedience to God
- nurtures a root of skepticism
- hinders prayer
- leads to instability
- feeds a critical attitude
- desensitizes God's people to the Holy Spirit and to spiritual things
- poisons others
- fosters arrogance and pride
- undercuts people's regard for God's Word and His character
- holds up my own standard as the correct standard, even placing it ahead of the Lord's standard
- brings discouragement to others and dampens their faith
- incurs God's disappointment, anger, and disfavor
- hinders the release and the activity of the Holy Spirit
- leads to control

RECOGNIZING UNBELIEF

Ask the Holy Spirit to examine your heart as you consider the following checklist. Check all that apply:

- ❏ I find myself being disappointed—even offended—that God doesn't seem to work as I believe He should, or answer my prayers in the way I'd like.
- ❏ When I hear of others' experiences of God's presence, power, or answered prayer, I am skeptical. My usual first reaction is to try to analyze or disprove their claim.
- ❏ I try to pass off a critical spirit as being a Berean spirit ("spiritually discerning" and "protecting"—see Acts 17:11).
- ❏ I am critical of the direction and methods of church and ministry leaders.
- ❏ I tend to be suspicious of others.

❏ I wonder why the Holy Spirit doesn't seem to talk to me or use me as powerfully as He uses others.

❏ I doubt that God really speaks to or uses others as they claim because I don't see Him speaking to me or using me in those ways.

❏ I tend to be self-sufficient and independent from others; if I'm honest about it, I tend to be self-sufficient and independent from God.

❏ I first perceive people and situations as impossible, rather than possible with God.

❏ I am not confident that I have spiritual authority through Jesus Christ.

❏ I am not motivated to pray consistently, and

❏ I have little interest in intercessory or spiritual warfare prayer.

❏ Prayer is usually a last resort for me. I try to figure things out or work them out for myself first. My actions would indicate I believe that God helps those who help themselves.

❏ I succumb to habitual behaviors and addictions (coping mechanisms) to comfort me when I feel discouraged, afraid, hopeless, hurt, etc.

❏ I make decisions based on my fears rather than on what I feel God wants me to do in a given situation (where to go, how to get there, what my spouse/children can do, or where they can go, etc.).

❏ I think my situation, my sins, my fears, my marriage, my spiritual life, my (you fill in the blank) will never change.

❏ I panic when I receive bad or distressing news, or even the suggestion that something bad or distressing may occur.

❏ I tend to be worried, fearful, and anxious about many things.

❏ I fear that my children or other family members will never be saved.

❏ I try to control people, situations, and even God, because I am afraid to let go and trust Him to care for them, to lead them, to protect them, to save them, etc.

❏ I am skeptical of the present-day supernatural work of the Holy Spirit.

❏ I fear taking the risk of praying and ministering boldly with others in areas like healing or spiritual freedom.

❏ I fear stepping out in faith in response to confirmed revelation God has given to me or to others in the body of Christ.

❏ Visible circumstances have a stronger influence on me than do the written Word, spoken words, or the character of God.

BREAKING FREE OF FEAR AND UNBELIEF

• Realize that behind every fear lurks a lie. Fear only takes root in us when we believe a deception about an anticipated danger, conflict, or pain. The problem is not the potential situation. The problem is the lie we believe about God's ability (or perceived inability) to protect, provide, comfort, strengthen, and equip us for every circumstance in life.

• You must make the decision to hate the sins of fear and unbelief with holy violence. Fear grieves God's heart, for it denies the reality of His awesome provision and protection. Fear fuels unbelief in God, His character, His Word, and His power.

118

- Confess all specific areas of the sins of fear and unbelief.
- Ask God to reveal any areas and root issues of fear that are still unknown to you. Consider asking someone to pray with you about this. They may have insight or receive Holy Spirit revelation about areas of fear that are blind spots to you.
- Renounce fear and unbelief in the name of Jesus, and rebuke the enemy by the name and blood of Jesus. Firmly command the enemy to go, and stand in faith (use the 4Rs).

Every time we take steps of faith and something supernatural happens, our faith—and our confidence—is reinforced. As faith grows, fear is diminished!

Then move "in the opposite spirit"—in the opposite direction—of your fears. It is not enough to confess your fears; now you must face them aggressively, receive God's love and promises, and replace all unbelief with confident affirmation of the truth of God's Word and character.

LIVING FREE OF FEAR AND UNBELIEF

As we grow in our willingness and ability to live in freedom, we are challenged to face areas in which we may have little or no previous experience. We look at our own physical, psychological, and emotional resources and realize they are inadequate or the demands of life, ministry, and spiritual battle. We begin to see the enormous gap between what we can do in our own strength (natural) and what we can do in the power of the Holy Spirit (supernatural).

That gap is bridged when we look not at our own hands and our own inadequacies, but when we step out in faith to do what Jesus said we would do, should do, and could do! Every time we take these steps of faith and something supernatural happens, our faith—and our confidence—is reinforced. As faith grows, fear is diminished!

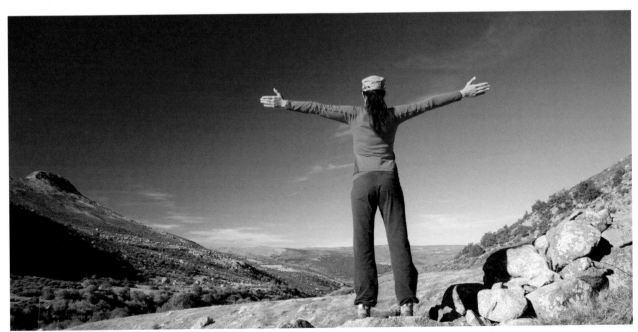

Make the following affirmations:

- ❏ I will renounce fear and doubt and replace them with faith and confidence in the Word, the character, and the power of God.
- ❏ I will not live only by what I see and understand with my natural senses or with my emotional reactions and fears, but according to the Word and revealed promises of God.
- ❏ I will always seek to honor Him, and I will not dishonor Him or those who are seeking to walk in obedience and in large faith.
- ❏ I will ask the Lord daily to increase my faith.
- ❏ I will spend more time in the Word so I can know God's work, character, and promises more fully.
- ❏ I will learn to hear His voice and to act on it.
- ❏ I will not live in rebellion by fearing the natural consequences of obedience to God.
- ❏ I will not hide an unbelieving, critical spirit under the guise of being practical, prudent, or "Berean."
- ❏ I will wait for God to fulfill His promises; I will not rely on my own schemes, false comforts, coping mechanisms, or control.
- ❏ I will step out boldly in faith to minister in ways that Jesus did.
- ❏ I will live and minister confidently in the spiritual authority that is mine through Jesus Christ.
- ❏ I will live above my emotions and circumstances, trusting fully in God to provide for, to protect, and to empower me.
- ❏ I will not fear or rebel against the supernatural work of the Holy Spirit.
- ❏ I will cultivate a culture of faith with those around me, beginning with my family, and including my ministry, my church family, and my friends.

SCRIPTURES TO LIVE BY

FEAR

Psalm 23:4 (NIV)
Even though I walk through the valley of the shadow of death, I will fear no evil, for you are with me; your rod and your staff, they comfort me.

Proverbs 12:25 (NIV)
An anxious heart weighs a man down, but a kind word cheers him up.

Isaiah 8:12 (NIV)
Do not call conspiracy everything that these people call conspiracy; do not fear what they fear, and do not dread it.

Isaiah 41:10, 13 (NIV)
So do not fear, for I am with you; do not be dismayed, for I am your God. I will strengthen you and help you; I will uphold you with my righteous right hand. For I am the LORD, your God, who

takes hold of your right hand and says to you, Do not fear; I will help you.

Matthew 28:20 (NIV)
Surely I am with you always, to the very end of the age.

Acts 18:10 (NIV)
For I am with you, and no one is going to attack and harm you, because I have many people in this city.

Philippians 4:6 (NIV)
Do not be anxious about anything, but in everything, by prayer and petition, with thanksgiving, present your requests to God.

UNBELIEF

Psalm 78 :19-22
They spoke against God, saying, "Can God spread a table in the desert? When he struck the rock, water gushed out, and streams flowed abundantly. But can he also give us food? Can he supply meat for his people?" When the LORD heard them, he was very angry; his fire broke out against Jacob, and his wrath rose against Israel, for they did not believe in God or trust in his deliverance.

Matthew 6: 25-30 (NIV)
That is why I tell you not to worry about everyday life—whether you have enough food and drink, or enough clothes to wear. Isn't life more than food, and your body more than clothing? Look at the birds. They don't plant or harvest or store food in barns, for your heavenly Father feeds them. And aren't you far more valuable to him than they are? Can all your worries add a single moment to your life? And why worry about your clothing? Look at the lilies of the field and how they grow. They don't work or make their clothing, yet Solomon in all his glory was not dressed as beautifully as they are. And if God cares so wonderfully for wildflowers that are here today and thrown into the fire tomorrow, he will certainly care for you. Why do you have so little faith?

Matthew 13:58
And he did not do many miracles there because of their lack of faith.

Hebrews 11:1
Now faith is being sure of what we hope for and certain of what we do not see.

Hebrews 11:6
And without faith it is impossible to please God, because anyone who comes to him must believe that he exists and that he rewards those who earnestly seek him.

INSIGNIFICANCE AND INFERIORITY

Martin Luther once reportedly said that it doesn't matter which side of the horse you fall off of—either way, you've fallen off the horse! That holds true for Satan's approach to separating us from the love of God. One way he does it is through convincing us that we don't need His love and forgiveness. We think we're okay just the way we are. That's pride.

But the other equally insidious scheme is to deceive us into thinking we don't deserve His love and forgiveness. In this case, we tear ourselves down. We focus on our insecurities and inadequacies, wallow in self-pity and self-hatred, and withdraw into a prison of rejection, condemnation, and insecurity. We call this stronghold insignificance and inferiority.

ROOTS OF INSIGNIFICANCE AND INFERIORITY

A stronghold of insignificance and inferiority filters our perception of reality with the lie that we are not loved and significant simply for who we are—and that we (and others) are only valued by our position, abilities, appearance, status, success, possessions, career, or ministry. We fail to recognize that we are unconditionally loved and valued by God. This stronghold sustains a vicious cycle of hopelessness, striving, and despair: hopelessness that we will never be and do the things we dream of, striving to make it all happen, and despair and condemnation when we fail.

RECOGNIZING INSIGNIFICANCE AND INFERIORITY

Insignificance is believing that we are lower in order (of less value, of less importance) and status than another, poorer in quality, or below average. It insists that God can't (or won't) bless us like He does others. It assumes this to be the reason things haven't worked out or have gone wrong, or why our prayers haven't been answered. Insignificance is rooted in lies and labels from the enemy, who has opposed you from birth.

- Insignificance is rooted in being overly conscious of yourself, and coming up short when comparing yourself against others.

- Insignificance causes us to struggle with self-pity, anger, and covetousness.

- Insignificance convinces us that we do not belong, and that we always get short-changed (self-pity). We can nearly always see how others are greater (or more significant) than we are in everything.

- Insignificance makes us believe that the Lord does not see us or smile upon us, and so we reject the promise that He has a purpose for us. We find no joy in the fact that He has chosen us.

- We live with buried anger toward people who represent groups in our past who rejected us, or who made us feel like we were second class. We are often critical of these people because they make us feel inferior. Anger will rise up against them in many diverse ways.

A stronghold of insignificance and inferiority filters our perception of reality.

ASK THE HOLY SPIRIT TO HELP YOU EXAMINE YOUR HEART AS YOU CONSIDER THE FOLLOWING CHECKLIST

I often feel and think (check all that apply):

- ❑ I am nobody from nowhere.
- ❑ I am ugly and weak and despised.
- ❑ I have nothing to give to anyone.
- ❑ I am not a "real" man/woman.
- ❑ I think people don't want to speak to me because they are superior to me.
- ❑ I look down when I walk by people.
- ❑ I don't say "hi" to people, because no one knows me and it seems that nobody cares.
- ❑ I am shy (or I am often labeled "shy") because I have nothing to say to others.
- ❑ Everyone in my family, including me, is a nobody.
- ❑ I don't see any good in who the Lord created me to be (ungratefulness).
- ❑ I dislike myself.

INSIGNIFICANCE BREEDS A HEIGHTENED AWARENESS OF SELF

- ❑ I am often self-conscious and internally focused.
- ❑ I often compare myself to others.
- ❑ I find myself wondering what others think about me, which leads to a deep sense of insecurity.

INSIGNIFICANCE SEES TO IT THAT WE ALWAYS FALL SHORT IN THE COMPARISON GAME WITH OTHERS

- ❏ I constantly compare myself to others, and I usually fall short.
- ❏ I fear speaking to people whom I regard as superior to me.
- ❏ I covet what others have (friends, marriages, children, boy/girlfriends, jobs, positions, possessions, physical appearance, skills, and abilities).
- ❏ I am jealous of what other people look like and how they act and speak.
- ❏ I only build friendships with those I regard as my equals or whom I regard as inferior to me.

INSIGNIFICANCE CAUSES US TO FEAR OR AVOID HEALTHY, GOD-GIVEN CHALLENGES INTENDED TO BRING NEW GROWTH IN OUR LIFE (PASSIVITY)

- ❏ I am relieved when another person is chosen for an assignment.
- ❏ I am fearful or anxious of being responsible for tasks, because I believe I will probably fail.
- ❏ I prefer to remain hidden and anonymous, and be passed over for assignments.
- ❏ I want to be given easy assignments I can accomplish with my natural abilities.
- ❏ I only choose to do things familiar to me.
- ❏ I only speak to people with whom I am familiar.
- ❏ I avoid risks (praying out loud, speaking in front of people, taking leadership or positions of responsibility).
- ❏ I am desperately afraid to fail, so I play it safe.
- ❏ I prefer being alone because it's safer, easier, and less work.
- ❏ I am unable or feel unfit to share the gospel with others ("It's someone else's job").
- ❏ If forced to engage in a risk-taking activity, I am eager for it to be over.

- ❏ If forced to participate in a risk-taking activity, I become tired and weary.
- ❏ I do not find joy in the Lord's challenges.

INSIGNIFICANCE RESTS ON HEAVY UNBELIEF ABOUT OUR AUTHORITY AND OUR GOD-GIVEN PLACE IN THE BODY OF CHRIST

- ❏ The Lord does not take my prayers seriously.
- ❏ It's hard for me to believe that God has chosen me for a significant purpose.
- ❏ I feel I am insignificant to the Lord.
- ❏ When a pastor speaks about being a "warrior for Christ," I feel he or she is not talking to me.

- ❑ I feel like no one knows me or sees me.
- ❑ The Lord doesn't speak to me.
- ❑ I often question God's presence in my life.
- ❑ I do not believe I have any authority or spiritual "punch;" everything I do is weak.
- ❑ I can't see my destiny (even when someone tries to point it out to me), or how I will be used to advance the kingdom of God.

INSIGNIFICANCE FINDS COMFORT IN SELF-PITY

- ❑ I blame others for not seeing anything good in me.
- ❑ My parents weren't very encouraging to me, so that is why I don't believe in myself.
- ❑ "These are just my character traits—God made me this way!"
- ❑ I am a victim of a hard life.
- ❑ No one ever blesses me, so don't expect much of me.

INSIGNIFICANCE BREEDS CRITICISM OF OTHERS WHO ARE DIFFERENT FROM US

- ❑ I am critical of others because I couldn't or wouldn't do things the way they do it.
- ❑ I am critical of others when they challenge me, because "I can't change."
- ❑ I am critical of others because I believe that they think they are superior to me.

INSIGNIFICANCE CAUSES US TO WITHHOLD BLESSING FROM OTHERS

- ❑ I withhold blessing from others because I have nothing to give.
- ❑ I withhold blessing from others because my thoughts/encouragements about others don't really matter to them.
- ❑ I withhold blessing from others because I do not want them to pass me up (I am threatened and insecure).

INSIGNIFICANCE SEEKS MAN'S APPROVAL

- ❑ I feel rejected if I am not encouraged or recognized.
- ❑ I do what I think others would like me to do.
- ❑ I say things I think will cause others to approve of me.
- ❑ I feel insecure if others think badly of me.
- ❑ I hate unresolved conflict.

INSIGNIFICANCE LEADS TO AMBITION

- ❑ I find it hard to cope with failure.
- ❑ Success is a very high priority for me.
- ❑ I judge myself and others by the measure of their success.
- ❑ I see success as something to be attained.
- ❑ I want people to think highly of me.
- ❑ I value my reputation.

Notes: _____

BREAKING FREE OF INSIGNIFICANCE AND INFERIORITY

REPENT

Jesus, I ask forgiveness for every way insignificance and inferiority have affected my life and the lives of those around me. (Specifically ask forgiveness for each box you checked as well as any sins that come to mind associated with each category.) I ask for Your forgiveness for walking in unbelief about the way You made me, and about Your great love and plans for me. I see it and call it sin. I now turn in repentance, committing myself to breaking the patterns of insignificance and inferiority in my life.

REBUKE

In Jesus' name and authority, I rebuke the spirit of insignificance. I take authority over every area of my life that I have given over to insignificance and inferiority. Every spirit of anger, jealousy, competition, self-pity, unbelief, rebellion, insecurity, and every deceiving spirit must go to the feet of Jesus. With the authority I have in Jesus, I renounce and rebuke in Jesus' name every spirit that would lie to me about who God is and what He says about me.

REPLACE

I replace the deceptions of the enemy with the truth of who God is and what He says of me. I choose to believe that I am precious, loved and chosen by God and that He withholds no good thing from me.

RECEIVE

Jesus, I receive Your promised forgiveness. I pray for and in faith receive the infilling of Your Holy Spirit to live a supernatural life. I recognize and receive my significance, Your love and favor toward me, how purposefully and intricately You created me, and the amazing purpose You have for me in my life.

LIVING FREE OF INSIGNIFICANCE AND INFERIORITY

To truly live free of the stronghold of insignificance and inferiority, we have to practically live out words and actions based on the reality of our acceptance and significance in Christ. Receive, affirm, and act on these truths!

God loves you deeply. It is an insult to Him when you belittle yourself and doubt your significance. Don't call "unclean" what God has called "clean." (Acts 10:15)

To truly live free of the stronghold of insignificance and inferiority, we have to practically live out words and actions based on the reality of our acceptance and significance in Christ.

God has honored you highly. He has adopted you, made you His child, and called you as a royal, holy priest in His kingdom (1 Peter 2:9-10). Live like it! Don't confuse self-deprecation with humility.

God values you greatly. While you were still a sinner, Christ died for you (Romans 5:8). In redeeming you, God declared your value to the heavenlies. Don't hang your head in worthlessness—you were bought at a great price.

God has provided for you fully. He delights in giving you good things. He never lets the righteous go hungry. He has given you the spiritual gifts you need to fulfill your calling and destiny. Don't be overwhelmed by your own inadequacy—He will supply your every need (Philippians 4:19).

God has planned for you carefully. He chose you from before the foundation of the world (read Ephesians 1). He's had a long time to think about you!

God has gifted you abundantly. When Jesus ascended from his victory over Satan at the Cross, He led a triumphant procession in the heavenlies, and distributed the plunder! Part of that booty is the spiritual gifts that He has distributed by the Holy Spirit to God's people, for warfare and kingdom building (see Ephesians 4:7-13). You have been given specific gifts for a specific purpose in that process.

God has delighted in you immeasurably. He even rejoices over you with singing! (Zephaniah 3:17). Remember what He said at Jesus' baptism? "…my beloved Son, in whom I am well-pleased." Scripture tells us over and over again that we are "in Christ." You are beloved. You don't have to prove yourself. The Father is well-pleased with you!

SCRIPTURES TO LIVE BY

Proverbs 14:30 (NIV)
A heart at peace gives life to the body, but envy rots the bones.

Jeremiah 29:11
"For I know the plans I have for you," says the LORD. "They are plans for good and not for disaster, to give you a future and a hope."

Romans 12:6
In his grace, God has given us different gifts for doing certain things well.

Ephesians 4:7
He has given each one of us a special gift through the generosity of Christ.

James 3:16
For wherever there is jealousy and selfish ambition, there you will find disorder and evil of every kind.

1 John 3:1
See how very much our Father loves us, for he calls us his children, and that is what we are! But the people who belong to this world don't recognize that we are God's children because they don't know him.

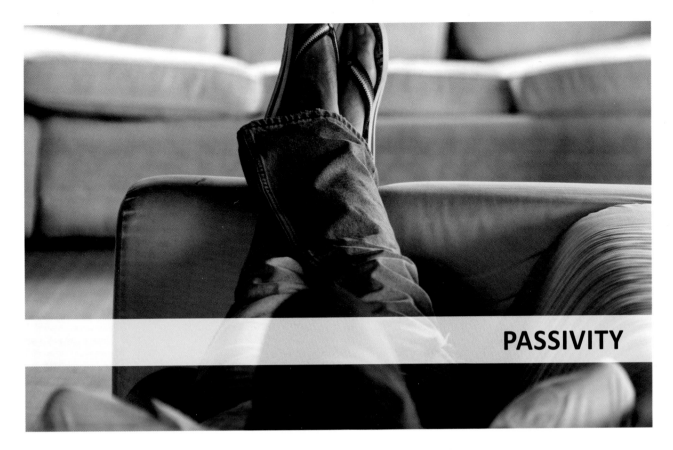

PASSIVITY

Jesus taught that the kingdom of God must be taken by force. "The kingdom of heaven has been forcefully advancing," He said, "and forceful men lay hold of it" (Matthew 11:12, NIV). Jesus wasn't talking about building God's kingdom through physical violence. He was talking about power, effort, initiative, and action.

The words "force" and "forceful" that Jesus used in this text of Scripture are the Greek words *biastes* and *biazo*, which mean "to press violently or force one's way into." The same word is used to refer to the "pounding of the surf" in Acts 27:41. As powerful waves beat relentlessly and unceasingly on the ocean shore, so our lives are to be powerfully persevering in our pursuit of and obedience to God.

In the "faith chapter" in the book of Hebrews, the writer talks of people whose faith transformed their weakness to strength—*dunamis*—the kind of strength we talked about in the chapter on God's authority and power (see Section Four in this manual). This transformation enabled them to become powerful in battle and to rout foreign enemies (Hebrews 11:34). With this kind of spiritual force and power, the passage goes on to say, some women even saw dead loved ones raised to life again (vs. 35)!

In order to truly live free of the enemy's assaults on our life, and in order for God's kingdom to advance in our lives and our world, we must move in the force, power, and authority of Jesus Christ. We are called (and empowered) to be "more than conquerors" in Him (Romans 8:37). The spirit of passivity, however, seeks to crush the force of Christ's power and authority in you. It seeks to render you weak, impotent, and useless. It attacks you at the core of God's original design for you—which is to be the bearer of His image and authority on earth.

Notes: _____

_____

_____

_____

_____

_____

_____

_____

_____

_____

_____

_____

_____

_____

_____

_____

_____

_____

ROOTS OF PASSIVITY

The spirit of passivity has a many-faceted approach to quenching the fire of God in you, but it always starts in the mind. Why do we not move more forcefully in life, relationships, activities, and ministry? Look for the following roots that energize passivity (or lack of initiation, activity, and obedience):

- Discouragement
- Faintheartedness, heaviness
- Depression
- Intimidation
- Self-indulgence
- Procrastination
- Various fears: fear of failure, fear of confrontation, fear of rejection, etc.
- Self-determination/rebellion/independence
- Laziness

RECOGNIZING PASSIVITY

Passivity is inactivity where godly obedience should be taking place. It can include allowing oneself to be unhelpfully acted upon, submitting without objection or resistance, hesitation on areas of biblical obedience, and lack of initiation.

- Passivity is not from the Lord, and is a form of rebellion.
- It occurs in the place where activity should be occurring.
- God calls us out of passivity. He calls us to be active in our faith, active in building relationships, active in service, and active in every area of our lives.

Proverbs 20:4
A sluggard does not plow in season; so at harvest time he looks but finds nothing.

Proverbs 10:4
Lazy hands make a man poor, but diligent hands bring wealth.

Hebrews 6:11-12
We want each of you to show this same diligence to the very end, in order to make your hope sure. We do not want you to become lazy, but to imitate those who through faith and patience inherit what has been promised.

Prayerfully consider the following checklists. Ask the Holy Spirit to expose any areas of passivity in your life. Check all that apply:

> *Passivity is inactivity where godly obedience should be taking place.*

PASSIVITY IS A FORM OF INDEPENDENCE AND LEADS TO ISOLATION

- ❑ I resist interdependence.
- ❑ I do not ask for help from the church body.
- ❑ I do not offer help/service to others in the church body.
- ❑ I see myself as more of a "private" Christian.
- ❑ I am reserved and keep to myself.
- ❑ I am critical of the way things are done in my church, and I have doubts about the leadership (I can see many flaws); it seems best for me to keep some distance and not get too involved.
- ❑ I tend to observe the activities of others (socially or in ministry); I rarely feel motivated or worthy to join in.
- ❑ I feel like I don't need anyone else.
- ❑ I do not feel worthy to be in relationship with others.

PASSIVITY IS A FORM OF RESISTANCE OR REBELLION

- ❑ I resist God's forgiveness by not taking the authority Jesus has given me over my sin.
- ❑ I resist obedience to the Lord by allowing sins to remain in my life.
- ❑ I do not seek the place of repentance.
- ❑ I have become familiar with, and indifferent toward, sins in my life.
- ❑ I do not believe it would do any good to take authority over sins in my life.
- ❑ I resist receiving the Lord's gifts.
- ❑ I do not believe that God would give me supernatural gifts and use them through me.
- ❑ I am not sure that spiritual gifts are authentic or for today; I want to keep a safe distance from them.
- ❑ I expect that others may receive gifts, but I won't.
- ❑ I resist leadership positions because I don't want that much responsibility or pressure.
- ❑ I don't like to do what everyone else does; I am my own person.
- ❑ It's not like me to get "more involved," and I don't want to be pressured to do so.
- ❑ It's not like me to be a leader or be assertive.
- ❑ If (that person) would just be quiet and let some others talk/lead/initiate once in a while, then maybe I would get involved (critical, judgmental spirit).

PASSIVITY ALLOWS SELF-PITY TO REMAIN

❑ I am familiar with feelings like fear and rejection, so I tend to believe that is the way things will be for me.
❑ I am comfortable with the way I am.
❑ I am a victim; I don't know how not to be a victim.
❑ Others are wrong to push me to become someone I am not. I blame others for the way that I am.

PASSIVITY IS ABOUT BEING TOO COMFORTABLE

❑ I allow myself to be comfortable with where I am spiritually. I'm all right with my walk with God right now.
❑ I allow myself to be comfortable with where I am emotionally. I have always struggled with _____ (for example, depression, insecurity, shyness, fear, loneliness, etc). This is the way things are, so why should I worry about it and try to find a "cure"?
❑ I allow myself to be comfortable with where I am physically. I don't care what others think of my appearance. Too bad if they don't like what they see.

PASSIVITY LIES TO US

❑ "I am not meant to step out and initiate or I would really 'feel like it.'"
❑ "I will be a failure if I try to initiate."
❑ "It's just not me!"
❑ "There is nothing wrong with me, so I don't need to seek change or freedom."
❑ "At least there is some comfort in self-pity and being a victim."
❑ "I don't need anyone telling me how to act!"

BREAKING FREE OF PASSIVITY

REPENT

Repent of every way you have walked in passivity—including ways you have used it to seek comfort, escape, and/or independence. Confess the section headings in the previous exercise and anything specific you believe needs to be addressed under each. Ask for—and receive—God's forgiveness.

REBUKE

Rebuke any and every demonic spirit of passivity that has assaulted and attacked you with lies about your true nature and calling, causing you to be passive in any areas of your life. Come against them by the authority of Jesus Christ. Put them under your feet according to the Word of God. Utterly reject them and the influence they have had in your life.

REPLACE

Replace the spirit of passivity with the truth of who God is and who He created you to be. Begin to live with initiative and passion toward the Lord and all that is right in Him—both toward Him and other people. Commit to breaking the patterns of passivity by taking initiative and being aggressive in your pursuit of Him and His ways.

RECEIVE

Receive God's forgiveness for the sin of walking in passivity. Accept His offering of cleansing from this sin and say that you are forgiven! Pray for and receive the infilling of the Holy Spirit to empower you to live a life that rejects passivity and embraces initiative and passion for God, His glory, the advancing of His kingdom, and obedience toward Him.

Breaking free of passivity requires that we move out of self-focus and into selflessness and abandonment to God.

LIVING FREE OF PASSIVITY

Breaking free of passivity requires that we move out of self-focus and into selflessness and abandonment to God. It also requires we exercise faith, and the power and authority that Jesus has given us. We put aside our good intentions, our self-indulgence, and our comfort-seeking ways to eagerly seek to obey God. We begin to actively bless, serve, and encourage people, to do the works and ministry of Jesus, and to overcome every scheme of the enemy.

Affirm the following truths and declarations in your own life:

- I will initiate conversations, activities, etc. with others. I will go to them and will not wait for them to come to me.
- Even when I don't feel like it, I will take authority over sin patterns such as self-pity and victimization. I will not allow sin to remain. I will use the authority Christ has given to me!
- I will do the things I know I ought to do, even when I really don't feel like it.
- I will go out of my way to bless, encourage, and serve people.
- I will not assume that someone else will take care of something. I will take responsibility and action.
- I will not confuse peacemaking and passivity. I recognize that inaction is not peace. Jesus was a peacemaker, but He always moved in forceful aggression (spiritually and practically) toward evil, injustice, and sin.
- I will make prayer and Scripture reading daily priorities in my life (not just good intentions).
- I will follow through with promptings of the Holy Spirit. I will not let myself off the hook by saying, "It was just my imagination," or "I'll do it later…"

- When the Holy Spirit convicts me of a sinful thought, word, action, or attitude, I will repent IMMEDIATELY and turn in the opposite direction. I will not tolerate sin in my life.
- When the Holy Spirit speaks to me and prompts me to share a word of encouragement, discernment, healing, or hope to someone, I will do it!
- I will honor my promises and commitments. If I tell someone I'll do something, I will do it!

SCRIPTURES TO LIVE BY

James 4:17 (NIV)
Anyone, then, who knows the good he ought to do and doesn't do it, sins.

Proverbs 20:4 (NIV)
A sluggard does not plow in season; so at harvest time he looks but finds nothing.

Hebrews 6:11-12 (NIV)
We want each of you to show this same diligence to the very end, in order to make your hope sure. We do not want you to become lazy, but to imitate those who through faith and patience inherit what has been promised.

Acts 20:34-35 (NIV)
You yourselves know that these hands of mine have supplied my own needs and the needs of my companions. In everything I did, I showed you that by this kind of hard work we must help the weak, remembering the words the Lord Jesus himself said: "It is more blessed to give than to receive."

1 Corinthians 9:24-25 (NIV)
Do you not know that in a race all the runners run, but only one gets the prize? Run in such a way as to get the prize. Everyone who competes in the games goes into strict training. They do it to get a crown that will not last; but we do it to get a crown that will last forever.

2 Timothy 2:6-7 (NIV)
The hardworking farmer should be the first to receive a share of the crops. Reflect on what I am saying, for the Lord will give you insight into all this.

REJECTION

We belong to a society that values winning and worships winners. We live under a world system that chooses favorites and rejects seconds. We learn, pretty much from birth, that the most popular, the most attractive, and the most talented are "in." Those who don't fit that description (most of us) are "out." And so, before even a specific action or attitude is leveled against us, the stage is set for each of us to live life battling rejection.

Rejection is foundational to many strongholds, sins, and dysfunctions. This is because rejection affects a person's entire personality. It not only comes against an individual, but it works against all of a person's relationships: marriage, family, ministry, work, and social life. When each of us begins to make our way in life, the stage is already set by the world system, which we know to be under the direction of Satan, the "accuser of the brethren" (Revelation 12:10). Where we yearn for love and acceptance, we often receive rejection instead. We learn to believe the lies fed to us about our own value, our own significance, and the love of God, our Heavenly Father.

However, if we are in Christ, we do not need to participate in this world system. We have not been rejected; we have been accepted (Romans 15:7). There is nothing that can separate us from the love of our Father (Romans 8:38-39), and we must not buy into the lies that tell us otherwise. Instead, we must face those lies squarely, identify what they are and where they come from, and destroy them utterly with the sword of the Spirit—which is the Word of God.

Notes: _____

ROOTS OF REJECTION

- Absent fathers or mothers
- Lack of bonding with parents
- Parents' divorce
- Not being wanted as a child; being the "wrong" gender
- Adoption
- Competition with siblings
- Various forms of abuse (physical, emotional, sexual)
- Parents' addictions
- Shame of a family member
- Constant fighting or strife
- Unjust discipline
- Disinterest in a child's activities
- Various means and degrees of neglect/abandonment
- Living with physical defect or handicap
- Discontent with one's appearance or abilities
- Infidelity of a spouse
- Divorce
- Breaking off of an engagement or other significant relationship
- Loss of valued employment
- Betrayal by a loyal friend
- Unexpected, premature death of a loved one
- Spiritual abuse, hurt, or betrayal in a church
- Racial prejudices
- Class distinctions

RESULTS OF REJECTION

- Causes people to rely on their own coping mechanisms (false comforts), instead of on the truth, power, and strength of God's Holy Spirit
- Breeds rebellion (rejection results in rebellion), including aggressive attitudes, foul language, stubbornness, defiance, fighting, and abusive actions
- Fosters pride, egotism, and arrogance
- Feeds control, manipulation, and possessiveness
- Compels people to reject others
- Causes people to refuse comfort from others
- Promotes harshness, scepticism, and unbelief
- Leads to self-rejection (low self-image, inferiority, insecurity, inadequacy, sorrow, grief)
- Causes self-accusation and self-condemnation
- Energizes an inability or refusal to communicate (it is difficult to talk through issues with a person who is suffering from deep rejection)
- Stirs up and feeds fears, anxieties, worries, negativity, and pessimism
- Spawns depression, hopelessness, and despair
- Triggers self-destructive thoughts and actions
- Fuels performance-based life, relationships, and ministry
- Energizes over-achievement, striving, competition, and perfectionism

- Drives people into withdrawal, isolation, or independence
- Nurtures self-protection, self-centeredness, selfishness, self-justification, self-idolatry, and self-pity (note that it's all about SELF!)
- Feeds a critical spirit, judgmental attitudes, envy, jealousy, and covetousness
- Keeps people locked in emotional immaturity

RECOGNIZING REJECTION

Prayerfully consider the following checklists. Ask the Holy Spirit to expose any areas of passivity in your life. Check all that apply:

Nothing can separate us from the love of our Father and we must not buy into the lies that tell us otherwise.

- ❑ I usually interpret things that could be either positive or negative as negative.
- ❑ I receive what others say to me through a lens of rejection.
- ❑ I second-guess what I have said or done, and I have negative thoughts about what others must think about me as a result.
- ❑ I find it difficult to freely reach out and exercise my spiritual gifts.
- ❑ I often try to "do too much" or go from thing to thing, job to job, ministry to ministry, striving to earn favor and acceptance from God and/or others.
- ❑ I find it difficult to accept freely from others, or to demonstrate love and affection.
- ❑ I don't believe people when they pay me a compliment.
- ❑ I have a tendency to doubt, question, or mistrust authority.
- ❑ I tend to be skeptical and unbelieving of other peoples' overtures of friendship or appreciation.
- ❑ People could describe me as harsh.
- ❑ I struggle to control foul language and abusive speech, especially when I am angry.
- ❑ When confronted about something, my immediate reaction is defensive or even defiant.
- ❑ I do not share my testimony, or the gospel, with the unsaved.
- ❑ I am afraid that I, or my loved ones, have not been chosen by God for salvation.
- ❑ I feel a need to control my family in order for them to be safe, to succeed, and so they will love and appreciate me.
- ❑ I am possessive in relationships.
- ❑ I have a low estimation of my own appearance, abilities, and adequacy to succeed in life and ministry.
- ❑ I am prone to depression.

- ❑ I am often fearful and anxious about things, such as how people will regard me or my children, how my efforts will turn out, and how I will be provided for and protected.
- ❑ I need to be needed, so I continually place myself in situations where I feel others cannot get along without my help, my presence, my abilities, and my ministry.
- ❑ I am inhibited in honestly sharing my deepest feelings with others, even with those who are close to me.
- ❑ I am afraid if I am vulnerable with my wife, my husband, my friend, or others (even those close to me), I will appear weak and lose my place of authority and respect in their eyes.
- ❑ I am afraid if I am vulnerable with my husband, my wife, my friend, or others (even those close to me), they will take advantage of me and exploit my weakness.
- ❑ I am both critical and envious at the same time toward others who are more confident, who are able to express themselves freely, or who have more friendships and opportunities than I think I do.
- ❑ I am competitive and ambitious. I think if people won't love me, at least they will admire me.
- ❑ I find comfort in isolation; others might consider me a "loner."

FALSE REJECTION

The rejection issues noted above have their roots in reality—the offenses that created the sense of rejection really did happen. Two forms of rejection that are not based in reality are perceived rejection and feared rejection. These are pure demonic lies convincing a person that rejection is present or pending when it is not. These can paralyze us in life, strip us of joy, and compel us to be always on guard against what others may be thinking.

PERCEIVED REJECTION

- ❑ I think people are always talking about me when they are not.
- ❑ I believe there are conspiracies against me when there are not.
- ❑ I usually interpret things that could be either positive or negative as negative.
- ❑ I receive what others say to me through a lens of rejection.

FEARED (SUSPECTED) REJECTION

- ❑ I am assaulted frequently with paralyzing thoughts such as, "I can't do that!"; "How would that appear to (person)?"; "What will (person) think if I wear this, do this, say that?"
- ❑ I am unable to freely reach out and exercise my spiritual gifts (to minister helps or mercy, to speak words of exhortation and encouragement, etc.).

138

- ❏ I do not experience intimacy with God in prayer or personal worship, because I think God will reject me.
- ❏ I am inhibited in corporate worship, because I am concerned about what others may think about me.
- ❏ I am often fearful and anxious about how I relate to other people, and they to me.
- ❏ I do not extend comfort or encouragement to others, even if I sense that they need it.
- ❏ I do not step out in faith and boldness, because I fear I might mess up, or that people won't receive what I have to offer.
- ❏ I end relationships before other people have a chance to hurt me.
- ❏ I am afraid to enter into a committed relationship with someone of the opposite sex out of fear of the break-up that I am sure will happen.

BREAKING FREE OF REJECTION

As you pray through the stronghold of rejection, identify and grant forgiveness and blessing to any offender(s), real or perceived. This may go all the way back to childhood. Do not feel that you have to deal with it all in one sitting. It may take several prayer times to deal with the stronghold of rejection. Use the 4Rs to help you pray:

REPENT

Repent of the ways that rejection and fear of rejection have marked your life, and the ways you have reacted with sin responses. Use the checklists on the previous pages to highlight these, and to help you as you confess them to the Lord.

REBUKE

Rebuke the enemy for his lies and his influence. Take authority over his schemes to deceive you and keep you locked down and isolated from the love of the Father and the people around you.

REPLACE

Replace the lies with truth, confidence, and security in God's love and acceptance for you. Affirm, out loud, the truths itemized below. Continually renew your mind by spending time in God's Word, in His presence through prayer and worship, and in the fellowship of your family, friends, and church family.

RECEIVE

Receive God's gracious forgiveness, and a fresh filling of His Holy Spirit. Ask Him to give you a new and very personal revelation of His great love for you. He delights to answer such a prayer.

> As you pray through the stronghold of rejection, identify and grant forgiveness and blessing to any offender(s), real or perceived.

Notes: _____

LIVING FREE FROM REJECTION

Grant forgiveness and extend blessings to people who have hurt or rejected you (real or perceived). Do the same toward situations and environments from which hurt and rejection continue to flow. Remember that Satan wants to stimulate bitterness, resentment, and anger in you. Your refusal to forgive hurts will become a toxin or a cancer that defiles not only yourself but also the people around you. This is why the Scriptures repeatedly address the issue of granting forgiveness.

Matthew 6:12, 14-15
Forgive us our debts, as we also have forgiven our debtors. For if you forgive men when they sin against you, your heavenly Father will also forgive you. But if you do not forgive men their sins, your Father will not forgive your sins.

Romans 12:20-21
On the contrary: "If your enemy is hungry, feed him; if he is thirsty, give him something to drink. In doing this, you will heap burning coals on his head." Do not be overcome by evil, but overcome evil with good.

Ephesians 4:31-32; 5:1-2
Get rid of all bitterness, rage and anger, brawling and slander, along with every form of malice. Be kind and compassionate to one another, forgiving each other, just as in Christ God forgave you. Be imitators of God, therefore, as dearly loved children and live a life of love, just as Christ loved us and gave himself up for us as a fragrant offering and sacrifice to God.

Be confident of God's great, unconditional, and infinite love for you. God did not make a mistake when He made you. His great love is demonstrated through Jesus' death on the cross and through His continual faithfulness and devotion to you. As you reject and demolish any strongholds and demonic lies of rejection, replace them with the truth of God's great love for you.

1 John 3:1
How great is the love the Father has lavished on us, that we should be called children of God! And that is what we are!

Live in these truths. This means acting on faith, not on feelings. It will mean behaving lovingly and confidently even when we fear people will reject us: parents, friends, children, co-workers, neighbors, and church family. It will mean forgiving and going on, even when they do reject us. This can include making and living out the following affirmations:

140

- I will immerse myself in the truth of God's word about who I really am: how much He loves me, accepts me, and demonstrates His faithfulness to me. I will not accept the lies of the enemy, perhaps planted into my mind and reinforced since childhood, that I am unloved, unaccepted, unworthy, or rejected.
- I will treat other people according to the truth of God's word, not on the basis of my own fears, hurts and insecurities. I will forgive. I will extend blessing. I will freely love and accept others.
- I will offer encouragement, blessing, and affection to others.
- I will express my thoughts and feelings to others honestly without fear of rejection.
- I will no longer resort to rebellion to express my anger over feeling rejected.
- I will no longer try to "do" for others so they will love and accept me. I will minister with my spiritual gifts according to the direction
- and power of the Holy Spirit.
- I will not fear weakness and vulnerability with my spouse. I will trust God to support me.
- I will not be critical of those who I feel have rejected me, or those who I regard as walking in greater freedom, acceptance, or
- confidence than me.
- I will form attitudes, initiate actions, and speak words that will comfort and encourage others.
- I will not seek comfort in self-pity or isolation.
- I will be myself, enjoying and becoming more comfortable with how God made me.
- I will share my faith in Jesus Christ whenever and with whomever the Holy Spirit gives opportunity.

SCRIPTURES TO LIVE BY

Psalm 13:1, 5-6
How long, O LORD? Will you forget me forever? How long will you hide your face from me? But I trust in your unfailing love; my heart rejoices in your salvation. I will sing to the LORD, for he has been good to me.

Psalm 27:1, 10
The LORD is my light and my salvation—whom shall I fear? The LORD is the stronghold of my life—of whom shall I be afraid? Though my father and mother forsake me, the LORD will receive me.

Psalm 66:20
Praise be to God, who has not rejected my prayer or withheld his love from me!

Isaiah 41:9-10

I took you from the ends of the earth; from its farthest corners I called you. I said, 'You are my servant'; I have chosen you and have not rejected you. So do not fear, for I am with you; do not be dismayed, for I am your God. I will strengthen you and help you; I will uphold you with my righteous right hand.

Isaiah 54:10

"Though the mountains be shaken and the hills be removed, yet my unfailing love for you will not be shaken nor my covenant of peace be removed," says the LORD, who has compassion on you.

Romans 5:8

But God demonstrates his own love for us in this: While we were still sinners, Christ died for us.

Romans 8:38-39

For I am convinced that neither death nor life, neither angels nor demons, neither the present nor the future, nor any powers, neither height nor depth, nor anything else in all creation, will be able to separate us from the love of God that is in Christ Jesus our Lord.

Ephesians 3:17-19

And I pray that you, being rooted and established in love, may have power, together with all the saints, to grasp how wide and long and high and deep is the love of Christ, and to know this love that surpasses knowledge—that you may be filled to the measure of all the fullness of God.

Isaiah 54:10

"Though the mountains be shaken and the hills be removed, yet my unfailing love for you will not be shaken nor my covenant of peace be removed," says the LORD, who has compassion on you.

SHAME AND HOPELESSNESS

Shame causes us to withhold ourselves in all areas of life. In its shadow, we tend to form shallow and guarded relationships. We do not move boldly and confidently in the power and authority that is ours in Jesus Christ. Instead, we live in fear that someone will find out how dirty or inadequate we really are (that is, that we *think* we are). Shame is like an unseen weight we drag through life.

This is not God's design for how His children should live. His Word tells us, "No one whose hope is in you will ever be put to shame" (Psalm 25:3, NIV). He wants us to bring our shameful burdens to Him and allow Him to lift them off us. But as long as our sins and our shame remain in the dark, they are a part of Satan's kingdom. He has jurisdiction over them—a legal right, so to speak. When we confess our sins and bring them out into the light, we break the hold Satan has over them. We are forgiven. We are cleansed. We are restored. We are made righteous. We are free!

1 John 1:9 (NIV)
If we confess our sins, he is faithful and just and will forgive us our sins and purify us from all unrighteousness.

Isaiah 61:10 (NIV)
For he has clothed me with garments of salvation and arrayed me in a robe of righteousness, as a bridegroom adorns his head like a priest, and as a bride adorns herself with her jewels.

Hopelessness is often related to shame. Hopelessness makes us feel like the pain, sorrow, discouragement, and condemnation we are feeling will never be lifted. We give up hoping for happiness. We give up hoping for true, lasting freedom. This, too, is a lie of the enemy.

Notes:

RECOGNIZING SHAME AND HOPELESSNESS

Definition of shame: painful feelings of guilt for improper behavior; associated with acts committed by a person as well as abuse committed against a person; usually carried in response to something hidden or kept secret. Related terms: disgrace; dishonor; deep feelings of embarrassment.

Definition of hopelessness: seeing no possibility to solve or overcome; having no expectation of a favorable outcome; despairing; despondent.

- Shame and hopelessness are often described as heavy baggage someone feels obligated to carry throughout life.
- Shame and hopelessness are not from God.

Psalm 25:3
No one whose hope is in you will ever be put to shame.

Psalm 43:5
Why am I discouraged? Why so sad? I will put my hope in God! I will praise him again—my Savior and my God!

- Shame is a result of sin.

Proverbs 13:18
He who ignores discipline comes topoverty and shame.

Jeremiah 8:9
The wise will be put to shame...since they have rejected the word of the Lord.

- Hopelessness is a result of not fully receiving and living in God's abundant love.

Romans 5:5
And hope does not disappoint us, because God has poured out his love into our hearts by the Holy Spirit, whom he has given us.

Check the boxes that apply to you:

SHAME

Shame causes us to develop only shallow, guarded relationships.

- ❑ I am afraid others might find out about this sin.
- ❑ I have trouble forming trusting relationships because I guard against getting "too personal" with others.
- ❑ I am very fearful that others can "see" my ugly sin—this causes me to fear drawing close to anyone, including God.
- ❑ I live in constant fear that others will reject me if this sin is discovered.

Shame results in a continuous battle with self-condemnation.

- ❑ I struggle with inferiority.
- ❑ I tend to think negatively about myself, and I battle negative thoughts about myself continuously.
- ❑ When I compare myself to others, I almost always lose the comparison.
- ❑ I beat myself up regarding this sin.
- ❑ I try to offset these condemning thoughts by pushing myself to succeed in other areas (work, school, athletics, etc). I somehow hope that doing this will disprove the condemning thoughts, but I never seem to make progress.

Shame brings deep feelings of guilt and unworthiness, which in turn lead to self-hatred.

- ❑ I feel dirty, ruined, or like "damaged goods."
- ❑ I have trouble finding intimacy with God because I feel so far from Him.
- ❑ I seem unable to forgive myself.
- ❑ I feel that I could never marry a godly man/woman because he/she might find out about this sin and reject me.
- ❑ I don't believe I can lead others because this sin has made me unworthy.
- ❑ I hate myself; I don't blame others for not wanting to be friends with me, because I don't deserve their friendship anyway.

Shame brings constant reminders (visions, memories) of this sin.

- ❑ I cannot stop thinking about this.
- ❑ I am constantly fighting off disturbing memories of my shameful experience(s).
- ❑ I have disturbing dreams and visions about this sin.

Shame robs us of the joy of forgiveness, and blocks the Lord's healing.

- ❑ I do not feel I can be forgiven for this sin.
- ❑ It is hard for me to believe that God can forgive even this.
- ❑ I cannot tell anyone about this, including God, because it is so shameful.

Shame lies to us.

- ❑ No one else has ever committed a sin as bad as this one.
- ❑ I have done the worst thing ever.
- ❑ I cannot tell anyone about this sin because they will reject me.

- ❑ I will never be clean.
- ❑ I will never be able to have deep relationships with others because I must make sure they never learn the truth about this sin.
- ❑ I am "damaged goods."
- ❑ I don't deserve a godly spouse.
- ❑ I am unworthy.
- ❑ I cannot lead others.

Note: Shame will keep its hold on you as long as you are afraid to specifically name those sins that brought shame. "Therefore confess your sins to each other and pray for each other so that you may be healed. The prayer of a righteous man is powerful and effective" (James 5:16, NIV). Before proceeding through the 4Rs, confess each area to one person.

Don't hold anything back. Generally speaking, men should confess to men and women to women. Because self-hatred is often a part of shame, ask God's forgiveness for this. When you have taken these steps, move on to the 4Rs.

HOPELESSNESS

Passivity adds to the weight of hopelessness.

- ❑ It's hard for me to spend time with God.
- ❑ During the day I find myself thinking, "What good would it do anyway?"
- ❑ I don't initiate conversations with friends, family members, or co-workers.
- ❑ I expect others to approach me and meet me where I am.
- ❑ I don't believe I am needed, so I give up on people or projects.
- ❑ I don't believe it would do any good to confess the sin in my life, so I don't.
- ❑ I have little passion for the things of God (evangelism, prayer, ministry, God's Word).
- ❑ I "allow" a lot of things to happen in my life.
- ❑ I think the idea of hope is a long shot.
- ❑ I lack motivation to pray or read God's Word.
- ❑ I lack motivation in most things in my life, or in things having to do with the Lord.
- ❑ I feel that sin will always have control of me, so there's little point in trying to overcome it.

Self-pity and introspection are at the center of hopelessness.

- ❑ Most of my thoughts are about me and what I can—and can't—do.
- ❑ A lot of people around me struggle with self-pity.
- ❑ To be honest, I don't have many close friends.
- ❑ My expectations of others are fairly high.

Hopelessness goes hand in hand with victimization and inferiority.

- ❑ I feel that there's little I can do about my own situation—it seems like I'm at the mercy of other people.
- ❑ I feel that my life is "locked in" because of what others have done to me.
- ❑ I do not like to share my friends with other people because I believe that those who are better than I am or have more than I do will steal them away.
- ❑ I feel protective and tight-fisted toward things and relationships because I fear someone will steal them from me.
- ❑ I don't feel free to share in a group because my comments or ideas would be pounded down or discounted.
- ❑ I am unable to step out with confidence or faith to break new ground.
- ❑ I rarely feel very sure of myself.
- ❑ I "play it safe" in life rather than risk what few resources (or confidence) I have.
- ❑ I resent it when the Lord lifts up others, because I feel that life has not been fair to me.
- ❑ I live a passive life. It's always someone else who makes things happen or leads the charge.

A lack of thankfulness creates openings for hopelessness to come in.

- ❑ I have a hard time thinking of things for which I can thank the Lord.
- ❑ I can't remember the last time I truly thanked the Lord for all of His provision in my life.
- ❑ I get locked down when I try to pray and to thank the Lord.
- ❑ Why should I give thanks when I have little or nothing to hope for?
- ❑ Sometimes I wonder if I will ever get out of this hopeless cycle.

Continuing on in a lifestyle of purity and holiness is a lifelong pursuit.

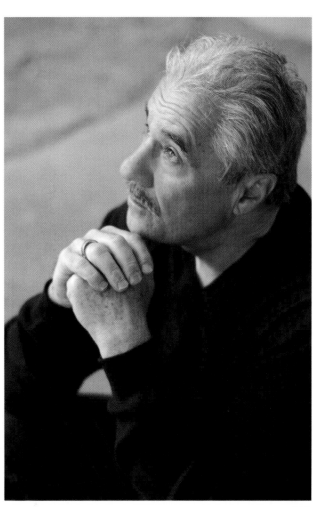

BREAKING FREE OF SHAME AND HOPELESSNESS

REPENT

Lord Jesus, I ask for Your forgiveness for this sin of carrying shame and/or hopelessness. I repent of all the ways I have allowed them to be a part of my life. I see how they have affected me and others around me. I name it as sin. Shame and hopelessness are not from You! (Go back through the boxes you checked and ask God to forgive you in each area.)

REBUKE

Lord, I renounce the life and ways of shame and hopelessness. That is not who I am and it does not represent You. I rebuke every evil spirit of shame for attacking me with thoughts of shame, disgrace, and unworthiness. I rebuke every spirit of hopelessness and despair that has tried to separate me from the love and life of my Heavenly Father. I come against them by the authority of Jesus Christ, and I command them to flee right now. They are liars, and I will no longer listen to them and their deceptions about me. According to the Word of God, I put them under my feet and I crush the influence they have had in my life.

REPLACE

I replace the life of shame with acceptance and recognition of being truly and fully a child of God. I replace hopelessness by living a life of joy, peace, courage, boldness, strength, authority, and love that will give a reason for the world to ask me about the reason for the hope in my life. I will live in the truth of courage, boldness, and confidence that rightfully belongs to those who are children of God.

RECEIVE

Lord Jesus, I now ask for and receive in faith the infilling of your Holy Spirit that I might live a supernatural life that lives above all shame and hopelessness. I walk in the hope, confidence, power, and authority that are mine as the child of the King of kings. I am accepted, and a living testimony of God's love, grace, and glory!

LIVING FREE OF SHAME AND HOPELESSNESS

Part of living free in Christ and walking in true purity and holiness depends on having our minds renewed by God's Word and His Holy Spirit. Refer to the resources at the back of this book, which are full of Scriptures that speak of God's love and forgiveness and of your true identity in Christ. Use the truth of God's Word and the authority you have in Christ to fight and renounce the lies of the enemy when they come back to torment your thoughts. Meditate on the promises of God about perfect forgiveness. This will cut down the lies that accuse you of being "unclean," and will be a source of comfort as well as a reminder of your true standing before the

Lord. Do not allow old mental videos, the words of others, and thoughts of worthlessness or guilt to define you. Those are not who you are!

Then you will need to make some choices. Continuing on in a lifestyle of purity and holiness is a lifelong pursuit; it doesn't just include behavior. It involves what we think, what we watch, what we speak, what we wear. These choices need to be made not out of a heart of legalism, though, but rather out of a heart restored and filled with God's Holy Spirit.

SCRIPTURES TO LIVE BY

Psalm 33:18 (NIV)
But the eyes of the Lord are on those who fear him, on those whose hope is in his unfailing love.

Psalm 119:114
You are my refuge and my shield; your word is my source of hope.

Isaiah 40:31
But those who trust in the LORD will find new strength. They will soar high on wings like eagles. They will run and not grow weary. They will walk and not faint.

Joel 2:26
Once again you will have all the food you want, and you will praise the LORD your God, who does these miracles for you. Never again will my people be disgraced.

Romans 15:13
I pray that God, the source of hope, will fill you completely with joy and peace because you trust in him. Then you will overflow with confident hope through the power of the Holy Spirit.

Romans 8:1
So now there is no condemnation for those who belong to Christ Jesus.

Ephesians 2:10
For we are God's masterpiece. He has created us anew in Christ Jesus, so we can do the good things he planned for us long ago.

THE CHRISTIAN'S BIRTHRIGHT

I am the light of the world, and the darkness cannot suppress it. **Matthew 5:14**

I am living in Christ's authority, which gives me power over all of the power of the enemy. **Luke 10:17-20**

I am part of the true vine, a channel of Christ's life and energy. **John 15:1, 5**

I am not condemned, but declared fully forgiven and righteous in Christ. **Romans 8:1**

I am a joint-heir with Christ, sharing His inheritance with Him. **Romans 8:17**

I am secure in Christ's love for me. **Romans 8:35-39**

I am an overwhelming conqueror in Christ against all that would come against me. **Romans 8:37-39**

I am a temple—a dwelling place of God. His spirit and His life dwell in me. **1 Corinthians 3:16; 6:19**

I am united to the Lord and am one spirit with Him. **1 Corinthians 6:17**

I am a member of Christ's body. **1 Corinthians 12:27; Ephesians 5:30**

I am a new creation in Christ, old things are passing away. **2 Corinthians 5:17**

I am reconciled to God and am a minister of reconciliation to God to others. **2 Corinthians 5:18-19**

I am righteous with God's righteousness. **2 Corinthians 5:21**

I am a child of God and one in Christ. **Galatians 3:26, 28**

I am a child of God, my personal heavenly Father, who intimately and infinitely loves me. **Galatians 4:6**

I am an heir of God since I am a child of God. **Galatians 4:6-7**

I am a saint. **Ephesians 1:1; 1 Corinthians 1:2; Philippians 1:1; Colossians 1:2**

I am seated in the heavenly realm, with Christ, in all His authority over Satan's kingdom. **Ephesians 1:19-23; 2:5-6**

I am God's workmanship, His handiwork, born anew in Christ to do His work. **Ephesians 2:10**

I am a fellow citizen with the rest of God's family. **Ephesians 2:19**

I am the light of God, and I expose the darkness by Christ's life in me. **Ephesians 2:19**

I am a warrior against Satan and fully outfitted to stand triumphant in Christ. **Ephesians 6:10-20**

I am hidden with Christ in God, so Satan must go through Christ to get to me. **Colossians 3:3**

I am an expression of the life of Christ because He is my life. **Colossians 3:4**

I am chosen of God, holy and dearly loved, and therefore jealously protected. **Colossians 3:12; 1 Thessalonians 1:4**

I am a holy partaker of a heavenly calling. **Hebrews 3:1**

I am a partaker of Christ; I share in His life. **Hebrews 3:14**

I am one of God's living stones, being built up in Christ as a spiritual house. **1 Peter 2:5**

I am a member of a chosen race, a royal priesthood, a holy nation, a people of God's own choosing. **1 Peter 2:9-10**

I am an alien and a stranger in this world in which I temporarily live. **1 Peter 2:11**

I am an enemy of the devil. **1 Peter 5:8**

I am a child of God and I will resemble Christ when He returns. **1 John 3:1-2**

I am born of God, and the evil one—the devil—must go through God to touch me. **1 John 5:18**

GOD'S LOVE AND FORGIVENESS

O give thanks to the Lord, for He is good; for His love endures forever. **1 Chronicles 16:34 (NASB)**

Many are the woes of the wicked, but the Lord's unfailing love surrounds the man who trusts in Him. **Psalm 32:10 (NIV)**

For great is Your love, reaching to the heavens; Your faithfulness reaches to the skies. **Psalm 57:10 (NIV)**

For great is Your love toward me; You have delivered me from the depths of the grave. **Psalm 86 :13 (NIV)**

But from everlasting to everlasting the Lord's love is with those who fear him, and his righteousness with their children's children. **Psalm 103:17 (NIV)**

Praise the Lord. Give thanks to the Lord, for he is good; his love endures forever. **Psalm 106:1 (NIV)**

Give thanks to the Lord, for he is good; his love endures forever... Let them give thanks to the Lord for his unfailing love and his wonderful deeds for men... Whoever is wise, let him heed these things and consider the great love of the Lord. **Psalm 107:1, 8, 43 (NIV)**

Praise the Lord, all you nations; extol him, all you peoples. For great is his love toward us, and the faithfulness of the Lord endures forever. **Psalm 117:1, 2 (NIV)**

The Lord is gracious and compassionate, slow to anger and rich in love. **Psalm 145:8 (NIV)**

Surely it was for my benefit that I suffered such anguish. In your love you kept me from the pit of destruction; you have put all my sins behind your back. **Isaiah 38:17 (NIV)**

The Lord appeared to us in the past, saying: I have loved you with an everlasting love; I have drawn you with loving-kindness. **Jeremiah 31:3 (NIV)**

Rend your heart and not your garments. Return to the Lord your God, for he is gracious and compassionate, slow to anger and abounding in love, and he relents from sending calamity. **Joel 2:13 (NIV)**

The Lord your God is in your midst, a victorious warrior. He will exult over you with joy, He will be quiet in His love, He will rejoice over you with shouts of joy. **Zephaniah 3:17 (NASB)**

For God so loved the world that he gave his one and only Son, that whoever believes in him shall not perish but have eternal life. **John 3:16 (NIV)**

For I am convinced that neither death nor life, neither angels, nor demons, neither the present nor the future, nor any powers, neither height nor depth, nor anything else in all creation, will be able to separate us from the love of God that is in Christ Jesus our Lord. **Romans 8:38-39 (NIV)**

But because of His great love for us, God, who is rich in mercy, made us alive with Christ even when we were dead in transgressions—it is by grace you have been saved. **Ephesians 2:4-5 (NIV)**

How great is the love the Father has lavished on us, that we should be called children of God! And that is what we are! The reason the world does not know us is that it did not know Him. **1 John 3:1 (NIV)**

They refused to listen and failed to remember the miracles you performed among them. They became stiffnecked and in their rebellion appointed a leader in order to return to their slavery. But you are a forgiving God, gracious and compassionate, slow to anger and abounding in love. Therefore, you did not desert them... **Nehemiah 9:17 (NIV)**

Praise the Lord, O my soul; all my inmost being, praise His holy name. Praise the Lord, O my soul, and forget not all His benefits—who forgives all your sins and heals all your diseases... **Psalm 103:1-3 (NIV)**

The Lord is compassionate and gracious, slow to anger, abounding in love. He does not treat us as our sins deserve or repay us according to our iniquities. For as high as the heavens are above the earth, so great is His love for those who fear Him;... for He knows how we are formed, He remembers that we are dust. **Psalm 103:8, 10, 11, 14 (NIV)**

Because of the Lord's great love we are not consumed, for his compassions never fail. **Lamentations 3:22 (NIV)**

WALKING IN THE OPPOSITE SPIRIT

Instead of anger:
- I do not let anger gain control over me; I think about it and remain silent. **(Psalm 4:4)**
- I do not let the sun go down on my anger. **(Ephesians 4:26)**
- I am prayerful and patient in the midst of trouble. **(Romans 12:12)**
- I do not pay back evil for evil, but I am patient and do good to everyone. **(1 Thessalonians 5:14)**
- I continue to show deep love for others, as love covers a multitude of sins. **(1 Peter 4:8)**
- It is Christ's love that controls me in whatever I do. **(2 Corinthians 5:14)**

Instead of control:
- I trust the Lord with all my heart, not leaning on my own understanding. **(Proverbs 3:5)**
- I do not control others, but I think of them as better than myself. **(Philippians 2:3)**
- I am gentle and show true humility to everyone. **(Titus 3:2)**
- I clothe myself with compassion, kindness, humility, and gentleness. **(Colossians 3:12)**
- I live in a manner that respects and submits to others. **(1 Peter 2:13-14)**
- I am the servant of others. **(Luke 14:43)**
- I will never be in want for anything because I know the Lord is my shepherd. **(Psalm 23:1)**

Instead of competing with others:
- I am a servant of Christ. **(Matthew 23:11)**
- In humility I consider others better than myself. **(Philippians 2:3)**
- I look out for the interests of others. **(Philippians 2:4)**
- I am a servant of all. **(Matthew 23:11)**
- I do good to all people. **(Galatians 6:10)**
- I am an encourager of others and I love my brothers and sisters in Christ. **(1 Thessalonians 5:14)**

Instead of criticizing others:
- I speak in a way that is helpful to others. **(Job 16:4-5)**
- I cover all offenses with love. **(Proverbs 17:9)**
- I do not judge or condemn others but only forgive. **(Matthew 7:1-2; Luke 6:37)**
- I bear the failings of those who are weak and purpose not to please myself. **(Romans 15:1)**
- I carry the burdens of others without comparing myself to them. **(Galatians 6:1)**
- I put on love and forgive all grievances I might have toward others. **(Colossians 3:13-14)**
- I am merciful, and speak and act without judgement. **(James 2:12-13)**
- I do not speak against, slander, or judge my neighbor. **(James 4:11-12)**

Instead of being fearful:
- I do not fear when the heat comes; my confidence is in the Lord. **(Jeremiah 17:7-8)**
- I am kept safe because of my trust in the Lord, and I will not fear man. **(Proverbs 29:25)**
- I have been given a spirit of power, love, and self-discipline, not fear. **(2 Timothy 1:7)**
- I have no fear of punishment because perfect love casts out fear. **(1 John 4:18)**
- I have no fear in my heart because the Lord protects me from danger. **(Psalm 27:1-3)**
- I am not afraid when I lie down because my sleep will be sweet. **(Proverbs 3:24)**
- I am not afraid of bad news; my heart is steadfast, trusting in the Lord. **(Psalm 112:7)**
- I am not afraid because the Lord is close beside me. **(Psalm 23:4)**
- I do not fear anything except the Lord. He will keep me safe. **(Isaiah 8:13)**
- I am no longer a slave to the fear of dying, for He will deliver me. **(Hebrews 2:14-15)**

Instead of feeling hopeless:
- I put my hope in God's word, for He is my refuge and my shield. **(Psalm 119:114)**
- I put my hope in God's unfailing love, and I know His eyes are upon me. **(Psalm 33:18)**
- I believe He delights in me because I put my hope in His unfailing love. **(Psalm 147:11)**
- I know that because I hope in God, He will renew my strength; I will soar on wings like eagles; I will run and not grow weary; I will walk and not faint. **(Isaiah 40:31)**
- I hope in the Lord, and He does not disappoint me. **(Isaiah 49:23)**
- I will not be disappointed, because God pours out His love into my heart. **(Romans 5:5)**
- I know that God gives me hope and will keep me happy and full of peace. **(Romans 15:13)**
- Since I have such hope, I am very bold. **(2 Corinthians 3:12)**
- I will overflow with hope through the power of the Holy Spirit. **(Romans 15:13)**

Instead of inferiority:
- I will not covet what others have. **(Exodus 20:17)**
- I am chosen by God to do the good works that He has prepared for me to do. **(Ephesians 2:10)**
- I am strong and I do not fear, for my God will come. **(Isaiah 35:4)**
- I am the salt of the earth and the light of the world. **(Matthew 5:13-14)**
- I am a spirit-powered witness of Christ. **(Acts 1:8)**
- I am God's workmanship. **(Ephesians 2:10)**
- I am highly favored by God, and He is with me. **(Luke 1:28)**
- I am a mighty warrior, and the Lord is with me. **(Judges 6:12)**
- I am confident of God's unconditional love for me. **(1 John 3:1)**
- I have been given a spirit of power, love, and self-discipline, and not fear. **(2 Timothy 1:7)**

Instead of insecurity:
- I am secure because nothing will separate me from the love of Christ. **(Romans 8:38)**
- I am complete in Christ. **(Colossians 2:10)**
- I have been chosen and appointed by God to bear fruit. **(John 15:16)**
- I may approach God with freedom and confidence. **(Ephesians 3:12)**
- The kingdom of God is within me. **(Luke 17:20-21)**
- He directs my path when I seek Him. **(Proverbs 3:5-6)**
- I am fearfully and wonderfully made. **(Psalm 139:10)**
- I am free from condemnation. **(Romans 8:1-2)**
- I am God's workmanship, created for good works. **(Ephesians 2:10)**
- I cannot be separated from the love of God. **(Romans 8:35-39)**

Instead of jealousy and envy:
- I am complete in Christ. **(Colossians 2:10)**
- I am assured that all things work together for good. **(Romans 8:28)**
- I have been chosen and appointed by God to bear fruit. **(John 15:16)**
- I am a temple of God. **(1 Corinthians 3:16)**
- I am God's workmanship, created for good works. **(Ephesians 2:10)**
- The Lord is my shepherd; I shall not want. He anoints my head with oil, my cup overflows. Surely goodness and love will follow me all the days of my life. **(Psalm 23:1, 5-6)**
- I am satisfied—I am fulfilled—I am full of joy and I am free.

Instead of passivity:
- I walk after the Lord my God and fear Him, and I keep His commandments and obey His voice. I shall serve Him and hold fast to Him. **(Deuteronomy 13:4)**
- I am diligent to the very end and am not lazy. **(Proverbs 10:4)**
- I work hard and show my love for God by loving and caring for others. **(Hebrews 6:10-11)**
- I have been chosen and appointed to bear fruit. **(John 15:16)**
- I am God's co-worker. **(2 Corinthians 6:1)**
- I can do all things through Him who strengthens me. **(Philippians 4:13)**
- I have not been given a spirit of timidity, but of power, love, and sound mind. **(2 Timothy 1:7)**
- I am not lazy, but I imitate those who through faith and patience inherit what has been promised. **(Hebrews 6:11-12)**

Instead of pride and arrogance:
- I hate pride and arrogance, evil behavior, and perverse speech. **(Proverbs 8:13)**
- I am wise to take advice from others because pride only breeds quarrels. **(Proverbs 13:10)**
- I choose to walk in humility and let God do the exalting. **(Luke 4:11)**
- I am the servant of others. **(Luke 14:43)**
- I do not boast about myself, but my approval comes from the Lord. **(2 Corinthians 10:10)**
- I love others. I do not boast; I am not proud or self-seeking. **(2 Corinthians 13:4-5)**
- I have humbled myself under God's mighty hand, and He will raise me up. **(1 Peter 5:6)**
- I am not selfish but think of others as better than myself. **(Philippians 2:3)**
- I do not live to make a good impression on others. **(Philippians 2:3)**

156

- I do not look to my own interests but only to the interests of others. **(Philippians 2:4)**
- I clothe myself with compassion, kindness, humility, and gentleness. **(Colossians 3:12)**
- I am gentle and show true humility to everyone. **(Titus 3:2)**

Instead of rebellion:
- I am obedient to God's truth and therefore am loved by Him. **(John 14:21)**
- I purpose to do nothing without consulting the Father. **(John 5:30)**
- I seek His will and not my own will on everything. **(Matthew 26:39)**
- I live in submission to those God has placed in authority. **(Romans 13:1-2)**
- I understand that those in authority have been placed there by God. **(Hebrews 13:7)**
- I live in a manner that respects and submits to others. **(1 Peter 2:13-14)**
- I honor all people and seek to support and protect their honor. **(1 Peter 2:17)**

Instead of rejection:
- I am confident of God's unconditional love for me. **(1 John 3:1)**
- I forgive and bless all those who have hurt or rejected me. **(Matthew 6:12; Ephesians 3:31-32)**
- I am loving and confident even when I fear people will reject me. **(1 John 4:18)**
- I am secure because nothing will separate me from the love of Christ. **(Romans 8:38)**
- I rejoice because the Lord has rescued me and has been so good to me. **(Psalms 13:1, 5-6)**
- I am not forsaken by the Lord, for He is the stronghold of my life. **(Psalm 27:1, 10)**
- I have been chosen by God and am not rejected. **(Isaiah 41:9)**
- I do not fear for He is with me to strengthen, help, and uphold me. **(Isaiah 41:10)**
- I know that the Lord takes great delight in me and rejoices over me. **(Zephaniah 3:17)**

Instead of shame:
- I will never be put to shame because I put my trust in Him. **(Romans 9:33)**
- I will never be put to shame because my hope is in Him. **(Psalm 25:3)**
- I will humble myself and pray and He will forgive my sin and heal me. **(2 Chronicles 7:14)**
- I look to Him and I am radiant; my face is never covered with shame. **(Psalm 34:5)**
- I have been given a new heart, and a new spirit has been put in me. **(Ezekiel 36:26)**
- I am in Christ Jesus; therefore there is no condemnation! **(Romans 8:1)**
- I will never again be ashamed, for God has worked wonders for me. **(Joel 2:26)**
- I am God's workmanship, created in Christ Jesus to do good works. **(Ephesians 2:10)**
- I am redeemed and forgiven of all my sins! **(Colossians 1:14)**

Instead of unbelief:
- I believe He exists and rewards those who earnestly seek Him. **(Hebrews 11:6)**
- I am sure of what I hope for and am certain of what I do not see. **(Hebrews 11:1)**
- I ask and believe without doubting because he who doubts is blown by the wind. **(James 1:6)**

- I take up the shield of faith and extinguish the arrows of the evil one. **(Ephesians 6:13, 16)**
- I live by faith and not by sight. **(2 Corinthians 5:7)**
- My faith does not rest in men's wisdom but in God's power. **(1 Corinthians 2:4-5)**
- I have faith in Jesus, and I will not only do what He did but greater things. **(John 14:12)**
- I will be among those He finds faithful when the Son of Man returns. **(Luke 18:8)**
- I will receive whatever I ask for in prayer because I believe. **(Matthew 21:22)**

Instead of unforgiveness:
- I forgive others, just as God in Christ also has forgiven me. **(Ephesians 4:32)**
- He forgives all my sins and heals all my diseases. **(Psalm 103:3)**
- He forgives my sins as I forgive those who sin against me. **(Matthew 6:12)**
- I forgive those who sin against me. **(Matthew 18:22)**
- If I hold anything against anyone, I will forgive him. **(Mark 11:25-26)**
- I say, "Father, forgive them for they do not know what they are doing." **(Luke 23:34)**
- I make allowances for others' faults and forgive those who offend me. **(Colossians 3:13)**
- I am merciful, thus God's mercy will win out over His judgment against me. **(James 2:13)**
- I confess my sins, and He is faithful and just to forgive and purify me of my sin. **(1 John 1:9)**

Instead of self-pity and victimization:
- I am secure because nothing will separate me from the love of Christ. **(Romans 8:38)**
- I believe He delights in me because I put my hope in His unfailing love. **(Psalm 147:11)**
- I know that the Lord takes great delight in me and rejoices over me. **(Zephaniah 3:17)**
- I forgive others just as God in Christ also has forgiven me. **(Ephesians 4:32)**
- I walk after the Lord my God, fear Him, keep His commandments, and obey. **(1 Samuel 12:14)**
- I am loving and confident even when I fear people will reject me. **(1 John 4:18)**
- I put my hope in His unfailing love, and I know His eyes are upon me. **(Psalm 33:18)**
- I am not selfish but think of others as better than myself. **(Philippians 2:3)**
- I do not look to my own interests but also to the interests of others. **(Philippians 2:4)**
- I am highly favored by God and He is with me. **(Luke 1:28)**

ENDNOTES

CHAPTER ONE:

1. This diagram is from the *Transforming Life* manual of St. Barnabas Church Kensington in London, England.

2. Adapted from the *High Octane Marriage Discipleship Manual* by Danny and Amy DeWalt, Sycamore Publications, Gig Harbor, WA: 2011. Used by permission. Available at www. sycamorecommission.org.

CHAPTER TWO:

1. Wayne Grudem, *Systematic Theology; An Introduction to Biblical Doctrine*, (Leicester: Inter-Varsity Press and Grand Rapids: Zondervan Publishing House, 1994), p. 782.

CHAPTER THREE:

1. Kittel, G., Friedrich, G., & Bromiley, G. W. (1995, c1985). *Theological Dictionary of the New Testament*. Translation of: Theologisches Worterbuch zum Neuen Testament. (187). Grand Rapids, Mich.: W.B. Eerdmans.

2. Arndt, W., Gingrich, F. W., Danker, F. W., & Bauer, W. (1996, c1979). *A Greek-English Lexicon of the New Testament and Other Early Christian Literature : A Translation and Adaptation of the Fourth Revised and Augmented Edition of Walter Bauer's Griechisch-deutsches Worterbuch zu den Schrift en des Neuen Testaments und der ubrigen urchristlichen Literatur* (277). Chicago: University of Chicago Press.

3. For more background on the heavenly war between the kingdom of God and the kingdom of Satan, refer to *Living Free: Recovering God's Design for Your Life* by Mike Riches, Sycamore Publications: Gig Harbor, WA, page 7-8.

CHAPTER SIX:

1. *Webster's New Twentieth Century Dictionary of the English Language*, ed. Jean L. McKechnie, (William Collins and World Publishing Company; 1977).

2. Merrill C. Tenney, ed., *The Zondervan Pictorial Encyclopedia of the Bible*, (Grand Rapids; Zondervan , 1975).

RESOURCES:

1. Jim Cymbala, *Fresh Faith,* Grand Rapids: Zondervan, 1999, 93.

LIVING FREE: RECOVERING GOD'S DESIGN FOR YOUR LIFE
by Mike Riches, 6X9", 262 pages
A narrative-style book giving a more in-depth explanation of the biblical truths and principles behind the *Living Free* course, packed full of real life stories

LIVING FREE COURSE COMPLETE CURRICULUM KIT
This three-DVD set (six sessions) features the *Living Free* course taught live by author Mike Riches and includes course manual, leader's guide, and DVD course facilitator's guide

LIVING FREE AVAILABLE IN FRENCH, GERMAN, AND SPANISH!

HIGH OCTANE MARRIAGE
by Danny and Amy DeWalt, 6X9", 240 pages
This book will get to the root of your marriage and release God's power for transformation and freedom. Get ready to overcome the pain of past wounds and patterns of distrust, experience new and lasting unity through repentance and forgiveness, speak the truth in love, break the power of secrets, and rebuild bullet-proof trust.

HIGH OCTANE MARRIAGE DISCIPLESHIP MANUAL
by Danny and Amy DeWalt, 8.5X11", 160 pages
A six-session manual to accompany the *High Octane Marriage* book. Great for churches and small groups, or for individual couples who want to dig more deeply into the powerful principles of "High Octane" marriage restoration.

HEARING GOD'S VOICE FOR YOURSELF AND OTHERS
by Mike Riches and Tom Jonez, 8.5X11", 96 pages
In this illustrated, full-color manual, you'll learn powerful truths and principles for returning to God's biblical normal for communicating with Him. Includes practical assignments for group or class study.

FREEDOM PRAYER TRAINING MANUAL "A"
by Mike Riches, 8.5X11", 96 pages
Freedom prayer ministry is a powerful way to apply the biblical truths of *Living Free* and *Hearing God's Voice*. This training will equip you to help people encounter God's love and truth and be released into the freedom God designed for His children.

SYCAMORE™ PUBLICATIONS

All products are available through the website
www.sycamorecommission.org